365 FOODS kids Love to eat

Nutritious and Kid-Tested!

Sheila Ellison & Dr. Judith Gray

SOURCEBOOKS, INC.®
NAPERVILLE, ILLINOIS

Published by: Sourcebooks, Inc.
P.O. Box 4410, Naperville, Illinois 60567–4410
(630) 961–3900
FAX: (630) 961–2168
www.sourcebooks.com

ISBN 1-4022-0585-6

The Library of Congress has catalogued the original edition as follows:
Ellison, Sheila.
365 foods kids love to eat : nutritious and kid-tested / by Sheila Ellison and Judith Gray.—Rev. 2nd ed. p. cm.
Includes index.
1. Cookery. 2. Children—Nutrition. I. Gray, Judith Anne, date. II. Title. III. Title: Three hundred and sixty-five foods kids love
to eat.
TX714.E45 1995
641.5¢622—dc20
95-3310

Printed and bound in the United States of America.
LB 10 9 8 7 6 5 4 3

Dedication

To the wonderful, healthy kids with whom I have shared food shopping, cooking, mealtimes, and cleaning up . . .

Jonathan
Andrew
Kirsty
Riki

—Judith

To my children Wesley, Brooke, Rhett, and Troy, for being my creative inspiration! To my brothers and sisters, Susan, Karen, David, Brian, and Brennan, who have shared mealtimes and memories.

—Sheila

Table of Contents

Chapter 21: Parties

Chapter 22: Holidays

Chapter 23: World Dishes

Introduction by the Authors

Families spend considerable time and energy on preparing food, putting it on the table, and supervising its consumption. Eating, especially for children, is a very important activity and one which enables them to develop social skills, communication skills, and self-esteem. Mealtimes, moreover, are opportunities for family bonding, sharing, interaction, relaxation, and learning consideration of others.

After many years of cooking for children and families, it occurred to us that today's parents needed a practical, comprehensive, easy-to-follow cookbook designed with kid's palates and appetites in mind. As our title suggests, our goal is to provide a sufficient range and variety of recipes so that you will be able to serve foods that your child will like and try year round.

We hope you will use this book when you are planning menus or when you are looking for recipes that balance or complement your meals or other food events. To that end we have included a sensible array of food sections, including snacks, fruits, salads, soups, breakfasts, and foods for your baby. Other sections focus on do-it-yourself ideas for kids, world dishes, lunch boxes, holidays, and children's parties.

Sheila Ellison   Judith Gray

Table Management for Families

✓ All family members should wash and dry hands before eating.

✓ Children should not be forced to eat what they don't want.

✓ Children should refuse foods tactfully and politely.

✓ If a food is not on the table, then it is not available.

✓ When serving your child's food, make sure the portions are small—she can always ask for seconds.

✓ The smaller the child, the slower he eats.

✓ Always have bread or rolls on the table.

✓ Instruct children to wipe their hands on a napkin, not on their clothes.

✓ Wait until *everyone* is seated before anyone commences eating.

✓ People bring food up to their mouths and animals take their mouths down to their food.

✓ Children can be temporarily excused from the table for nose blowing, coughing, or to go to the bathroom.

✓ Adults at the table should avoid monopolizing the conversation.

✓ Parents are the chief role models for children when it comes to manners and eating.

✓ Establish regular meal times.

✓ Establish times for snacks too.

✓ Children should come to the table reasonably hungry.

✓ Ban the expressions: "Yuck!" "Do I *have* to eat this?" "Gross!" and "What *is* this?"

✓ NO gum chewing at the table.

✓ Adults should not use mealtime to discuss matters that only concern them.

✓ Make an attempt to have something on the table that your child likes.

✓ Allow children to select the food they want from the table.

✓ Be considerate of everyone else at the table.

✓ Make sure that family eating is enjoyable and eagerly anticipated by all.

Healthful Suggestions

✓ Trim fats from meats and poultry before cooking.

✓ The yolk of an egg contains all the fat. Try using one egg yolk with 2 or more egg whites.

✓ Replace ground beef wherever possible with lean ground turkey.

✓ Buy products made naturally: Peanut butter, preserves, mayonnaise, and ketchup.

✓ Pure maple syrup is an excellent substitute for sugar.

✓ Spend some time reading labels and looking for pure foods and all-natural ingredients.

✓ Whole grain breads, cereals, flours, and baking mixes are important—they have more fiber.

✓ Avoid using baking powder that contains aluminum.

✓ Use canned skim milk in sauces, soups, and other recipes that call for cream.

✓ Most children love peanut butter—try other natural nut butters for variety.

Healthful Substitutions

✓ 1 teaspoon baking powder *equals* ½ teaspoon each cream of tartar and baking soda

✓ 1 square baking chocolate *equals* 3 tablespoons cocoa plus 1 tablespoon butter **or** 3 tablespoons carob plus 2 tablespoons water

✓ 1 cup sugar *equals* ¾ cup honey or 1¼ cups molasses **or** ¾ cup pure maple syrup

✓ 1 cup white flour *equals* ¾ cup whole wheat flour **or** ¾ cup graham flour or 1 cup whole wheat pastry flour

✓ 1 cup butter *equals* 1 cup margarine **or** ⅞ cup vegetable oil

✓ 1 cup buttermilk *equals* 1 cup milk plus 1¾ tablespoons cream of tartar

✓ 2 eggs *equal* 1 egg plus 2 egg whites **or** 2 tablespoons oil plus 1 tablespoon water

✓ 1 cup milk *equals* ½ cup evaporated milk plus ½ cup water **or** 3 tablespoons powdered milk plus 1 cup water

✓ 1 cup sour cream *equals* 1 tablespoon lemon juice **or** vinegar and 1 cup evaporated milk **or** 1 cup plain yogurt **or** 1 cup buttermilk

✓ 1 cup whipped cream *equals* 1 cup nonfat milk powder whipped with 1 cup ice water **or** 1 four ounce (125 g) package non-dairy whipped topping

Rules for Baby Food Chefs

✓ Breast milk or formula provides all the nutrients a baby needs for the first 4 months.

✓ Fish and soy products can cause allergies so are not recommended until baby is at least 8 months old.

✓ Egg yolks should not be given until 8 months and egg whites not until 12 months.

✓ Honey is not recommended for babies under one year—it is a potential source of bacteria that could make baby very sick.

✓ Yogurt and cheese may be added after 6 months.

✓ Ordinary cow's milk should not be given until baby is at least 6 months old. Leave the baby on breast milk or formula as long as you can.

✓ Dilute fruit juice ¼ fruit juice to ¾ boiled water.

✓ Beans are a good alternative to meat. Soak them for 8 hours, drain off soaking liquid then put in a pan, cover with water and simmer until soft. Then puree.

Making Your Own Baby Foods

✓ Food needs to be cooked sufficiently (medium soft) so that it can be easily pureed.

✓ Use a food processor or blender to puree the food.

✓ If food is dry after pureeing add one of the following: a little liquid from the vegetable, breast milk, formula, boiled water, or fruit juice.

✓ Don't add salt or sugar to any baby food.

✓ Prepare vegetables by peeling and cutting into small pieces. Cook in as little water as possible, steaming is best. Then put into the food processor or blender.

✓ To prepare fruits for cooking, peel and chop into small pieces then steam and put through a food processor or blender.

✓ Meat can be introduced in the form of saltless gravy, or juices added to baby's vegetables and pureed together.

✓ Cut meat into small pieces and place in a little boiling water. Simmer until cooked, then puree.

✓ Freeze what you don't use in meal-size portions. Ice cream trays work well for freezing. Once frozen, put frozen lumps into a freezer bag.

baby foods

Mashed potatoes
Pears and peas
Squished bananas
Bits of cheese

Vanilla yogurt
Jell-O too
Yellow squash
From Mother's stew

Delicious foods
Don't take up space
They all appear
On baby's face!

pear and spinach puree

Ages: 4 months and up

Ingredients
Fresh or frozen chopped spinach
   (however much you want)
1 pear peeled, cored, and diced
1 teaspoon butter

Directions
Simmer spinach gently in butter over low heat until warmed through.
Meanwhile, cook pear in a little boiling water until mushy. Drain, mash
into the spinach with a fork and serve warm.

Note: Some researchers believe that if you introduce vegetables before
fruits, children will enjoy vegetables more later on.

1

brown rice cereal

Ages: 4 months and up

Ingredients
1 teaspoon rice flour
4 ounces milk (breast or formula milk
   until about 6 months old)

Directions
Mix 1 ounce of the gently warmed milk slowly into the flour to make a paste, gradually adding the rest of the milk stirring continuously to avoid lumps. Simmer for 5 to 7 minutes. If it becomes too thick, add more milk. For variety, mix cereal with vegetable water or mashed vegetables, fruit purees or juices. Flaked millet, powdered oats, and later, semolina can all be used in a similar way.

Note: It is advisable to begin with rice and progress slowly through the other cereals: barley, millet, corn, oats, and finally, wheat. Many children have an allergic reaction to the gluten in wheat which is why it is usually wise to delay its introduction.

orange and sweet potato

Ages: 4 months and up

Ingredients
1 sweet potato
1 teaspoon butter
½ orange

Directions
Peel, chop, and boil sweet potato in a little water, drain and then mash with a little butter. Squeeze orange into sweet potato and stir. If baby is 9 months or older, add peeled, finely chopped orange segments.

Note: Try wrapping pieces of fruit in clear, sterilized muslin secured with a rubber band, for baby to chew on.

3

apricot and apple puree

Ages: 4 months and up

Ingredients
½ cup dried apricots
2 sweet apples
*Can use less of these ingredients
if you do not want to freeze.*

Directions
Rinse the dried apricots, then cover with cold water and soak overnight.
Simmer gently in the same water for about 25 minutes or until very soft
and pulpy. Cool. In the meantime, peel and core apples. Cook the sliced
apple in a little water or apple juice until it is soft. Puree the apricots
and apples. Freeze leftovers in ice cube trays.

Note: If possible, buy dried fruit which has been naturally dried and is
unsulfured. If fruit has been sulfur dried, the fruit needs to be washed
in hot water or soaked and drained before use.

peas pudding

Ages: 4 months and up

Ingredients

4 ounces (100 g) yellow split peas, washed and soaked overnight
½ small onion, cut in half
1 small parsnip, peeled and roughly sliced
1 carrot, peeled and roughly sliced
Sprigs of fresh parsley and thyme
1 pint water
1 ounce (25 g) butter

Directions

Before soaking the peas overnight, rinse them in several changes of cold water, then cover with fresh water. Using the water the peas were soaked in, make up to one pint with fresh water. Put this in a saucepan with the peas, onion, carrot, parsnip and herbs. (All the vegetables will be removed later so do not chop finely.) Bring to a boil, then lower the heat and simmer for about 45 minutes or until the peas are mushy and very tender. Drain off the water and remove the vegetables and herbs, leaving the peas in the pan. Add the butter and beat into a soft puree with a spoon. Serve warm.

Note: This is a traditional British dish served to adults as well. Try adding cooked brown rice and serving to the whole family.

homemade yogurt

Ages: 6 months and up

Ingredients
3 tablespoons commercial plain yogurt starter
2 tablespoons nonfat dry milk
2½ cups milk
Large glass jar

Directions
Prepare jar by pouring boiling water into it and letting it stand for a few minutes before emptying. (Put a spoon into jar to ensure that it doesn't break.) Mix the dried and whole milk and heat in a saucepan carefully until it almost reaches a boil. Set aside to cool until milk is just warm. Mix in commercial yogurt starter and pour into prepared jar. Screw on lid and wrap jar in a piece of clean blanket and place it in a plastic bucket. Put the bucket in a warm spot in the house and let stand for 6 hours. Unwrap and refrigerate.

Note: How yogurt works: Bacteria live on the sugar in the milk and break it down into lactic acid which causes the milk to curdle and become like junket. As soon as the yogurt is the right thickness it must be placed in the refrigerator where the coldness stops the further growth of bacteria. If the milk is not chilled quickly enough, the curds separate and the yogurt becomes watery. If the milk is kept too warm, the bacteria are destroyed and the milk doesn't thicken into yogurt.

yogurt plus

Ages: 6 months and up

Directions
Banana Yogurt: Mix a mashed banana with homemade yogurt.

Apple Yogurt: Mix 3 tablespoons plain yogurt with 2 tablespoons applesauce. Place ingredients in a blender and puree. Any fruit puree may be used.

Carob Yogurt: Mix 2 tablespoons plain yogurt with 1 teaspoon carob powder (8 months). Sprinkle carob over yogurt, mix and serve.

Yogurt Ice: Mix yogurt with any fruit puree in season and pour into ice cube trays. Partially freeze then add sticks; freeze until firm. (Keep a close eye on the sticks and take as soon as baby finishes.)

Wheat Germ Breakfast: (Don't give wheat germ to babies under 6 months): 1 tablespoon wheat germ, 2 tablespoons plain yogurt, 1 teaspoon maple syrup, 1 tablespoon pureed raw apple or mashed banana. Mix all ingredients together and serve.

Note: Yogurt can be made with whole milk, skim milk, nonfat dry milk, evaporated milk, even soybean milk.

basic oatmeal

Ages: 5 months and up

Ingredients
½ cup rolled oats, unground
2½ cups boiling water

Directions
Pour oats slowly into boiling water. Cover and simmer 30 minutes. Add milk or formula for desired consistency. As with all cereals, any fruit, vegetable or meat puree can be added.

Note: Make your initial cereal mixtures very moist when baby is first beginning to eat solids. You can increase thickness as baby gets used to the new texture.

8

corn cereal

Ages: 8 months and up

Ingredients
¼ cup yellow cornmeal
¼ cup cold water
2 teaspoons wheat germ
¾ cup boiling water
¼ cup nonfat dry milk (optional)

Directions
Mix together the cornmeal, cold water, and wheat germ. Add cornmeal mixture and nonfat dry milk to the boiling water. Stir constantly, bringing to a boil, then simmer for 2 minutes. Serve with pureed fruit.

vegetable puree

Ages: 4 months and up

Ingredients
Any vegetable you would like

Directions
Peel and chop vegetable into small pieces. Steam or boil them in as little water as possible until they are tender, then blend them with the cooking liquid left over. Mash with a fork or put in food processor or blender.

Note: Here are some great tasting foods to add to your vegetable puree for babies 6 months and older: cottage cheese, plain yogurt, egg yolk and wheat germ. To make a soup, just add extra milk, formula, or vegetable cooking water.

pumpkin bake

Ages: 6 months and up

Ingredients
1 cup cooked, mashed pumpkin
½ cup cottage cheese
1 tablespoon wheat germ

Directions
Preheat oven to 350°F (180°C). Butter a small ovenproof dish. Combine pumpkin and cheese and place in dish. Sprinkle wheat germ over the top and bake in oven for 10 minutes.

Note: Wilted, bruised or old vegetables have lost much of their vitamin C, so look for fresh vegetables even if they cost a bit more. Buy the vegetables that are in season and eat them as soon as possible. Avoid canned vegetables whenever possible. Buy organic vegetables whenever possible.

vegetable custard

Ages: 6 months and up

Ingredients
¼ cup pureed vegetables
(sweet potato, pumpkin, carrots or squash)
1 egg yolk, beaten
¼ cup milk or formula

Directions
Preheat oven to 375°F (190°C). Blend together ingredients and pour into a buttered ovenproof dish or individual custard cups. Place dish in a pan with 1 inch water in it and bake for 30 minutes.

Note: Wherever milk is called for soybean milk could also be used.

baked apple and potato pie

Ages: 6 months and up

Ingredients
¾ cup cooked sweet potato
1 red apple, peeled and sliced
¼ cup milk, or vegetable water
Wheat germ

Directions
Preheat oven to 350°F (180°C). Butter a small ovenproof dish. Layer apple slices and potato slices in alternate layers. Pour liquid over the top and sprinkle with a little wheat germ. Cover and bake for 30 minutes. Mash with a fork before serving. The rest of the family will enjoy this dish also—just leave out the mashing part!

spinach cheese bake

Ages: 8 months and up

Ingredients
½ cup cooked spinach
1 cup cooked mashed potato
1 tablespoon grated cheese

Directions
Preheat oven to 350°F (180°C). Wash spinach thoroughly and discard the stems. Place spinach leaves in a saucepan with very little water and cook 5 minutes. Drain and then puree. Combine the spinach, potato and cheese and place in a buttered ovenproof dish. Bake 15 minutes.

scrambled eggs plus

Ages: 12 months and up

Ingredients
1 egg
1 tablespoon milk
1 teaspoon butter

Directions
Beat egg and milk together in a small bowl or cup. Melt butter in a saucepan, pour in egg mixture and stir until egg is set.

Note: Scrambled eggs add needed protein and most kids love them. Try the following additions: cottage cheese, grated cheese, finely chopped leftover cooked vegetables, grated apple, chopped parsley, or mashed tomato with skin removed.

15

chicken with apples

Ages: 8 months and up

Ingredients
1 apple, peeled, cored and sliced
1 chicken breast, skinned and boned
½ cup apple juice

Directions
Simmer chicken and sliced apple gently in apple juice until both are tender. Puree in a blender. Serve warm.

Note: Meat and poultry provide iron and other valuable nutrients. Iron is the first nutrient that breast milk cannot supply in sufficient quantities as the baby grows.

chicken or beef stew

Ages: 8 months and up

Ingredients
1 boneless chicken breast or
   1 pound lean beef, cubed
1 cup chicken or beef stock
1 potato, diced
1 carrot, diced
½ cup peas
1 tomato, peeled
Any vegetable could be added

Directions
Place all ingredients in a covered saucepan and simmer gently for 30 minutes until tender. Puree until the texture is smooth and serve warm. This freezes well, so make extra.

baked custard

Ages: 12 months and up

Ingredients
1 egg
1 teaspoon honey
1 cup milk

Directions
Preheat oven to 300°F (150°C). Butter a small ovenproof dish. Beat the egg and honey together then add milk and pour into prepared dish. Place the dish in a baking pan half full of water (this prevents the custard from curdling while it is cooking. Bake for 15 to 20 minutes or until set.

couscous with cauliflower and carrots

Ages: 6 months and up

Ingredients
4 carrots, peeled and finely chopped
1 cup finely broken cauliflower florets
1½ cups low sodium chicken broth
1½ tablespoons unsalted butter
1 cup couscous
Sea salt

Directions
In a medium saucepan with a steamer, bring 2 inches of water to the boil. Add the carrots and cauliflower to the steamer and steam for 10 to 12 minutes or until the vegetables are tender. Drain and set vegetables aside. Heat the broth in the saucepan over medium heat. Melt the butter in another saucepan over medium-high heat and then add the couscous, stirring to coat will with the butter, and cook for 1 minute. Add the broth, cover and cook over medium heat for 4 minutes until the broth is absorbed. Stir in the vegetables and season with a little salt. Serve slightly warm. Yield: 4 servings.

beverages

Red and purple berries
Ice cubes that are pink
Swirls of green whipped cream
Mixed up in this drink.

Blended thick and frosty
Best served with a lunch
How I love this recipe
for "ROBIN'S RAINBOW PUNCH!"

cranana crush

Ingredients
1 banana, peeled and sliced
1 cup cranberry juice
⅓ cup orange juice
5 ice cubes

Directions
In a blender or food processor, combine the banana, cranberry juice, orange juice and ice. Cover and process until smooth. Yield: 2–3 servings.

Note: Have children do as much of the food preparation as they can. Children learn best by doing. Keep tasks age-appropriate to encourage success.

watermelon whirl

Ingredients
1 cup watermelon chunks, seeded and chilled
¼ cup unsweetened red grape juice
1 scoop plain ice cream
½ cup crushed ice
1 or 2 drops red food coloring

Directions
Place watermelon, grape juice, and ice cream in a blender jar and process until smooth and thick. Place the crushed ice in a tall glass. Pour the blender mixture over the ice. Gently stir in the food color. Use a pink or white straw and serve. Yield: 2 servings.

Note: Children need firm limits. Setting limits is a gift of love. Limits are the foundation of security. Kids who are lucky enough to have limits placed upon them in loving ways are secure enough to build self-confidence and are less likely to act up or misbehave.

chocolate frosted shake

Ingredients
1 cup low-fat milk
3 scoops chocolate ice cream
1 tablespoon chocolate syrup
Chocolate sprinkles (optional)

Directions
Put all ingredients in a blender. Process until thick and smooth. Pour into a tall glass and garnish with chocolate sprinkles. Yield: 1 serving.

Note: Keep a visible record of your child's growth. Attach a yard (meter) rule or a dressmaker's tape to the doorway of the kitchen. With a felt pen, regularly mark your child's height and add the date. Children like to be compared with other siblings, so use a different color for each family member.

cranberry delight

Ingredients
3 cups (12 ounce bag) cranberries
2 sticks cinnamon
3 cups prepared frozen orange juice
2 teaspoons lemon juice
¾ cup honey or sugar

Directions
Place cranberries in a saucepan and cover with water. Put in the cinnamon sticks and boil gently until berries are soft (about 5 to 8 minutes). Remove the cinnamon sticks. Strain the berries through a colander, crushing slightly. Set berry pulp aside. Add the prepared orange juice, lemon juice, and sweetener. Stir until sugar is dissolved. Add more water to make a gallon (2 liters). Simmer for 15 minutes. Serve hot in a mug or cup over a slice of lemon. Yield: 8 servings.

Note: Put the saved berry pulp in a small pan with ¾ cup sugar. Low boil for 10 minutes and voilá—a tasty cranberry sauce!

veggie refresher

Ingredients
½ cup carrot juice
½ cup tomato juice
Celery stick
Water to taste

Directions
Blend the carrot and tomato juices and add water to desired taste and consistency. Stir with a celery stick which can be nibbled between sips. Yield: 1 serving.

Note: Raw vegetable juices are good for children's general health and vitality. If you do not have a vegetable juicer, you can purchase a variety of prepared juices from organic food stores and from the produce section of your supermarket.

yogurt fruit shake

Ingredients
1 cup nonfat fruit flavored yogurt
(or plain yogurt with 3 tablespoons unsweetened jam added)
1 cup favorite fruit juice
1 cup ice cubes or 1 cup frozen fruit

Directions
Place all ingredients into a blender and blend until smooth. Eat with a spoon, a low-fat slushy delight! Yield: 2 servings.

Note: Yogurt is an ancient drink prepared from milk curdled by bacteria. In India, for instance, fresh yogurt is made daily by saving a little of the drink, adding milk and letting it sit in a warm place overnight while it thickens and sours. It is an excellent substitute for sour cream.

strawberry banana smoothie

Ingredients
1 ripe banana, peeled and sliced
6 fresh or frozen strawberries
1 cup plain or frozen yogurt
½ cup fruit sherbet
Ground nutmeg (optional)

Directions
Put all ingredients into a blender. Whirl until smooth. Serve in tall glasses and garnish with a slice of fresh fruit or a sprinkle of ground nutmeg. Yield: 2 servings.

hot cocoa nightcap

Ingredients
1 teaspoon cocoa powder
1 tablespoon honey or 2 teaspoons sugar
1 cup milk
A few drops vanilla extract

Directions
Put cocoa, honey or sugar, and one tablespoon milk in a cup and stir until smooth and shiny. Gradually pour in remaining milk. Heat in microwave oven for 2 minutes or until hot, but not boiling. Add vanilla, stir, and enjoy. Hot cocoa can also be prepared in a small saucepan. Be sure to stir constantly while heating milk. Serve with a cookie or graham cracker before bed . . . but remember to brush teeth! Yield: 1 serving.

Note: A warm drink before bed is said to promote sleepiness and relaxation. By the end of the day, most children also welcome some quiet time and a bedtime story.

strawberry fizz

Ingredients
1 cup frozen strawberries
½ cup low-fat milk
1 can diet strawberry soda

Directions
Place all ingredients in a blender and whirl until smooth. Pour into glasses and serve immediately. Other soda flavors can be used instead of strawberry for a fruitier taste.

Note: Help children identify and use kitchen utensils and equipment. Start with cutting boards, measuring cups, wooden spoons, graters, measuring spoons and plastic storage containers.

hot apple zinger

Ingredients
1 cup natural apple juice
1 cup water
10 cinnamon red hot candies
5 whole cloves

Directions
Heat the ingredients until the red hot candies dissolve. Simmer for 5 minutes. Strain and serve warm or cold. Yield: 2 servings.

Note: Did you know that the apple tree belongs to the rose family of plants? Crab apples look a lot like rose hips, the fruit of roses.

lemonade

Ingredients
3 lemons
½ cup honey or sugar
1 cup very hot water
3 cups cold water
Ice cubes
Fresh mint leaves

Directions
Cut lemons in half and squeeze the juice out of them. Put the juice and the honey into a pitcher. Add the cup of hot water and stir until the honey is dissolved. Add the cold water and ice cubes and stir. Rinse the mint leaves. Pour lemonade into glasses and garnish with mint leaves. Yield: 4 servings.

Note: This drink is a much healthier alternative to store-bought packets of lemonade mix.

For pink lemonade, add a drop of red food coloring to pitcher and garnish with slices of fresh strawberries.

simple egg nog

Ingredients
2 eggs
¼ cup honey
Pinch of salt
4 cups cold milk
1 teaspoon vanilla extract
Yellow food coloring

Directions
Beat or blend the first 4 ingredients until smooth. Add the vanilla and one drop of food coloring. Keep in the refrigerator until ready to drink. Can be heated slowly and served warm when it's cold outside. Yield: 4 servings.

sherbet party punch

Ingredients
4 cups fruit juice
2 cups soda water
1 pint (500 ml) frozen sherbet
Fruit garnishes

Directions
Mix together fruit juice and soda water in a punch bowl. Carefully place the sherbet in the bowl and stir until partially melted. Ladle punch into glasses or cups and garnish with strawberries, orange slices, pitted cherries or pineapple chunks. Yield: 8 servings.

minted lemon granita

Ingredients
4 cups cold water
40 mint leaves, washed
6 lemons
6 oz sugar
1 egg white

Directions
Peel the rind off the lemons and set aside. Squeeze and then strain the juice from the lemons. Pour water into a saucepan and add lemon rind and sugar. Heat gently until sugar dissolves, then bring mixture to the boil. Boil briskly for 5 minutes. Remove from heat and add lemon juice and mint leaves. Leave mixture to infuse for 15 minutes. Strain into a clean shallow dish. Place in the freezer and allow to partially freeze (3–4 hours). Remove dish from freezer and break icy pieces into flakes with a fork. Return to freezer. Repeat the breaking up process several times until the mixture has the consistency of loose ice crystals. Beat egg white until it holds its shape then fold into granita. Serve in chilled glasses and top each one with a sprig of mint leaves and a twist of lemon rind. Yield: 6 servings.

sun tea

Ingredients

3 tea bags (caffeine-free fruit
   or herbal teas are best)
1 gallon glass jar
Honey or sugar to taste
Flavorings:
Crushed mint leaves
Thin lemon slices
Cinnamon stick
Cloves

Directions

Fill the jar with cold water. Drop in the teabags, keeping the strings on the outside. Cover opening and place jar in a sunny spot for 4 hours. Remove teabags and add a flavoring. Chill. Serve over ice cubes and sweeten to taste.

Note: Tea is an ancient drink that originated in China. In the 4th century BC it was used as an aid in Buddhist meditation. Iced tea was introduced to America in 1904 at the St. Louis World's Fair.

breads
and muffins

Ripe bananas squished in honey
melted butter, soft and runny
watch her with a silly grin
dribbling batter tin to tin
created by our baby, Jan.

native american flat bread

Ingredients
4 cups unbleached flour
1¼ cups water
2 teaspoons baking powder
Pinch of salt
Vegetable oil or shortening

Directions
Mix the floor, one cup water (add the rest of the water only if it is needed), baking powder, and salt until well blended. Knead the dough for one minute. Cover and let rise for 20 minutes. Stretch and pat the bread out to a half-inch thick oval. Cut the oval into wedges, making a 1-inch slice in the middle of each wedge. Or have your child make a design on top of each wedge. Pour oil, ¾ inch high, into a large skillet. Fry wedges until golden brown. Serve with honey, jelly, or butter.

magical cinnamon rolls

Ingredients
1 package frozen bread dough
4 tablespoons butter
¼ cup sugar
¼ cup brown sugar
2 teaspoons cinnamon
½ cup raisins, optional

Frosting
½ cup powdered sugar
3 tablespoons milk

Directions
Thaw dough to room temperature and let rise overnight or until dou-bled. Pat dough into an 8x12-inch rectangle. Spread with the melted butter. Combine the sugar and cinnamon and sprinkle over butter. Evenly distribute the raisins over the top. Starting with longer side, roll up. Seal edges tightly. With a sharp knife, cut roll into 1-inch (20 cm) pieces. Place rolls flat side down on a greased cookie sheet, allowing room to spread, and let rise in a warm place until light and doubled in size. Bake at 375°F (190°C) for 20 minutes. Remove from oven and while still warm, drizzle with frosting or honey. Yield: 24 rolls.

popovers

Ingredients

1 cup milk
1 cup flour
2 eggs
¼ teaspoon salt
6 cold, greased custard cups

Directions

Put all the ingredients into a bowl. Stir until just blended. Don't bother to smooth out the lumps. Pour into a cold, well buttered custard cups (deeper than muffin tins, can be found at baking supply stores). Fill cups half full. Place the pan in a cold oven, then set the oven for 450°F (230°C) and the time for 30 minutes. Don't open the oven until the 30 minutes is up. Kids love to see how puffy these get, then how they sink when they are pulled open.

very berry muffins

Ingredients

2 cups flour
4 teaspoons baking powder
¾ cup sugar
1 teaspoon salt
1 cup fresh or frozen or canned berries (drained)
   blueberries or tart cherries work best
2 eggs
½ cup melted butter
1 cup milk
Cinnamon sugar for topping
   (⅛ teaspoon cinnamon to ½ cup sugar)

Directions

Preheat oven to 400°F (200°C). Sift flour, baking powder, sugar and salt together. Add berries and mix until well-coated. In a small bowl, beat eggs well and add melted butter and milk. Quickly stir liquid mixture into dry mix. Stir just until blended. Fill muffin cups ¾ full. Sprinkle a ½ teaspoon of cinnamon sugar on top of each muffin. Bake for 20 minutes or until brown. Yield: 12–14 muffins.

Note: Thanks to the Fisher family in Cedarburg, Wisconsin, who run a wonderful restaurant called Boders On-the-River, for sharing this recipe.

date scones

Ingredients
3 cups unbleached flour
4 teaspoons baking powder
Pinch salt
2 ounces (50 g) butter
1½ cup milk
½ to ¾ cup pitted dates

Directions
Preheat oven to 450°F (230°C). Sift dry ingredients into a medium bowl. Cut or rub butter into the flour mixture. Chop the dates and add. Make a hole in the middle of the dry mixture and pour in milk. Mix quickly to a soft dough with a knife. Turn out onto a floured surface and knead into a rectangle, 12x9 inches. Roll or pat to half-inch thickness. Cut into 12 to 16 squares and place close together on a greased cookie tray. Bake for 12 to 15 minutes. Yield: 12–16 scones.

best banana bread

Ingredients

2¼ cups unbleached flour, sifted
1 teaspoon baking powder
⅛ teaspoon salt
1 teaspoon baking soda
½ cup butter
1¼ cup sugar
2 beaten eggs

3 ripe bananas, pulped
2 beaten eggs
¾ cup sour milk
(buttermilk or regular milk
with 3 teaspoons lemon
juice added to it)

Directions

Preheat oven to 350°F (180°C). Sift together the dry ingredients and set aside. Blend butter, sugar and milk until creamy. Add the beaten eggs and banana pulp and stir until thoroughly mixed in. Add the dry ingredients and stir briefly. Dollop the batter into two greased and floured loaf pans. Bake in the center of the oven about 45 to 50 minutes. Test with a toothpick. Do not over cook. Cool before slicing. Yield: 2 loaves.

Note: Young food tastes need shaping. Dr. Story of the University of Minnesota School of Public Health suggests offering children as many nutritious choices as possible, serving sweets sometimes but never as rewards or bribes. Children can learn to eat well.

zucchini bran muffins

Ingredients
2 cups bran cereal
1 cup shredded zucchini
¾ cup milk
1 egg
½ cup sugar
⅓ cup vegetable oil
1½ cups unbleached flour
2 teaspoons baking powder
½ teaspoon each ginger and cinnamon

Directions
Preheat the oven to 375°F (190°C). In a large bowl, mix together bran cereal, zucchini, milk, egg, oil, and sugar. Set aside. Sift together flour, baking powder, and spices and then add to bran mixture. Stir until just moistened. Drop batter into 12 well-greased muffin pans about ¾ full. Bake for 30 minutes or until muffins are brown on top and firm to the touch. Serve warm or cool on wire rack. These muffins can be wrapped in airtight plastic wrap and frozen. Serve with butter or cream cheese. Yield: 24 muffins.

hansel and gretel gingerbread

Ingredients
2½ cups unbleached flour
2 teaspoons baking soda
1 teaspoon cinnamon
1 teaspoon ginger
1 teaspoon mixed spice
1 teaspoon cocoa
1 cup milk
½ cup light molasses
½ cup sugar
½ cup butter or margarine

Directions
Preheat oven to 350°F (180°C). Sift together all the dry ingredients in a large bowl. In a small saucepan or in the microwave oven, warm the milk, molasses, sugar and butter, stirring frequently. Do not boil. Cool and add to dry ingredients. Stir until blended, but do not over stir. Pour into a greased and floured loaf pan. Bake for 40 minutes or until toothpick comes out clean. Yield: 1 loaf (24 small servings).

Note: Encourage children to brush and floss their teeth promptly after meals. If that is not always possible, have them eat an apple or chew a sprig of parsley. The apple helps remove food particles and the parsley freshens the breath.

corny corn muffins

Ingredients

1 cup cornmeal
1 cup unbleached flour
2 teaspoons baking powder
3 tablespoons honey
1 egg, beaten
1 cup milk
¼ cup vegetable oil
Small can of corn, drained

Directions

Preheat oven to 425°F (220°C). Sift all the dry ingredients together into a medium bowl and set aside. Add the milk and oil to the beaten egg. Stir this mixture into the dry ingredients and add the corn. Do not over stir. Heat the muffin pans. Drop a little butter into each pan. Spoon into pans, ¾ full. Bake 15 to 20 minutes. Yield: 24 muffins.

Note: Cornbread mixes can be used to make these muffins. Remember, however, that they contain a lot more sugar.

cinderella's pumpkin bread

Ingredients
1 cup cooked or canned pumpkin
½ cup vegetable oil
2 eggs beaten
½ cup brown sugar
½ cup white sugar
2 cups unbleached flour
1 teaspoon baking soda
½ teaspoon each nutmeg and cinnamon
1 cup raisins (optional)
¼ cup water

Directions
Preheat oven to 350°F (180°C). Beat together the eggs, oil, pumpkin and sugars. Sift together the dry ingredients and add to pumpkin mixture. Stir in raisins and water and mix gently. Pour into a greased and floured loaf pan. Bake 1 hour or until a toothpick comes out clean. Wait 10 minutes before turning out onto a wire rack to cool. Yield: 1 loaf (24 small servings).

savory cheese muffins

Ingredients
2 cups unbleached flour
3 tablespoons grated Parmesan cheese
3 tablespoons grated Romano cheese
2 teaspoons baking powder
¾ teaspoon dill weed
Pinch salt
⅛ teaspoon garlic powder
1 cup milk
¼ cup vegetable oil
1 egg, beaten

Directions
Preheat oven to 400°F (200°C). In a bowl, combine flours, cheeses, baking powder, dill weed, salt, and garlic powder. Make a hole in the middle and add milk, oil, and egg. Stir just until dry ingredients are moistened. Spoon batter into baking cups, filling ¾ full. Bake 18 to 20 minutes or until golden brown. If desired, during last 3 minutes top each muffin with a teaspoon of grated cheddar cheese. Yield: 20 muffins.

Note: Paper baking cups can be used in conventional or microwave ovens. Use a double layer of cups when microwaving. Foil cups are generally easier to remove after baking than paper cups.

oatmeal raisin bread

Ingredients
1 packet active dry yeast
½ cup milk
1 cup cold water
¼ cup butter or margarine
¼ cup honey
1 cup raisins
2 cups instant uncooked oats
4–6 cups unbleached bread flour
1 teaspoon salt

Directions
Dissolve yeast in ¼ cup of warm water. Combine milk and cold water and heat until scalded. Pour hot liquid over butter, honey, raisins and salt in a large bowl and stir until butter melts. Cool until lukewarm. Add the yeast mixture and the oats. Beat in 2 cups of the flour until mixture is smooth. Add the remaining flour and stir to make a soft dough. Turn out onto a lightly floured surface and knead until elastic, about 10 minutes. Place in a greased bowl then turn upside down. Cover and let stand in a warm place until double in size. Punch dough down and place on floured surface. Shape into 2 loaves. Place in greased loaf pans, cover and let rise until nearly double. Bake at 375°F (190°C) for 45 minutes or until golden brown. Cool on racks. Yield: 2 loaves.

yogurt fruit scones

Ingredients
2⅔ cups unbleached flour
1/4 cup honey or sugar
1 teaspoon baking powder
6 tablespoons chilled butter, cut into small pieces
1 egg
1 egg, separated
1 cup plain yogurt
1 tablespoon water
1 cup raisins, dried cranberries or
other dried fruit, cut into small pieces
½ cup strawberry jam (unsweetened)

Directions
Preheat oven to 400°F (200°C). Grease baking sheet. Combine first 3 ingredients in a large bowl. Using a pastry blender or two knives, cut in butter until mixture resembles coarse meal. Mix whole egg and yolk. Stir into batter. Blend in yogurt. Turn mixture out onto lightly floured surface. Knead until dough comes together. Roll into a 9-inch circle, the dough being about 1 inch thick. Make knife marks on the top of the dough resembling a cut pie. Bake 12 minutes or until browned. Serve warm with jam and tea.

corn and tomato bread

Ingredients

3 large ears of fresh corn, shucked
1¾ cups yellow cornmeal
1 cup all-purpose flour
½ cup sugar
1 teaspoon baking powder
1 teaspoon sea salt
1 teaspoon baking soda
1 large egg
2¼ cups buttermilk
¼ cup diced and drained tomatoes

Directions

Preheat oven to 400°F (200°C). Lightly coat an 8-inch square baking pan with vegetable oil or butter. Cook the corn in boiling water for 5 minutes or until tender. Drain and run under cold water until cool enough to handle. Scrape the kernels off the cobs with a sharp knife and set aside. In a bowl, mix the cornmeal, flour, sugar, baking powder, salt, and baking soda. Whip together the egg and buttermilk and add to the flour mixture. Fold in the tomatoes and 1 cup of corn kernels. Set the baking pan in the oven until it begins to smoke. Remove and pour in the batter. Bake for 35 minutes, until golden brown or until a toothpick inserted into the center comes out clean. Allow the bread to cool for 20 minutes and invert to remove. To serve, cut into squares. Yield: 8–12 servings.

peanut butter mini muffins

Ingredients
3 ounces (75 g) cream cheese
¼ cup peanut butter
2 tablespoons honey
1 egg
1 cup unbleached flour
½ cup sugar
1 teaspoon baking soda
¼ teaspoon salt
⅔ cup milk
¼ cup vegetable oil
½ teaspoon vanilla extract
24 miniature foil baking cups

Directions
Preheat oven to 350°F (180°C). In a small bowl, combine the cream cheese, peanut butter, honey, and beaten egg. Beat until smooth and set aside. In a medium bowl, mix together flour, sugar, baking soda, and salt. Add milk, oil, and vanilla extract. Beat until smooth and spoon batter into the baking cups (about ¾ full). Top each with a teaspoon of the cream cheese mixture. Place cups on a cookie sheet and bake 20 to 25 minutes. Yield: 24 servings.

apricot carrot loaf

Ingredients
1 cup dried apricots
1⅓ cups unbleached flour
1 teaspoon baking powder
¼ teaspoon salt
½ teaspoon cinnamon
½ cup vegetable oil
2 eggs
¾ cup sugar
1 teaspoon vanilla extract
1 cup shredded carrot
¼ cup apricot preserves

Directions
Preheat oven to 350°F (180°C). Grease and flour a loaf pan. Chop apricots finely. Sift the dry ingredients into a bowl. Set aside. In another larger bowl, beat together the oil, eggs and sugar until fluffy and lemon colored. Add vanilla. Stir in dry ingredients and mix until smooth. Blend in the carrots and apricots. Pour into the prepared pan. Bake one hour or until a skewer inserted in center comes out clean. Invert onto wire rack to cool. In a small saucepan, warm the apricot preserves with 1 tablespoon water. Use a pastry brush to apply glaze to top of loaf. Yield: 16 servings.

breakfast

Every Sunday morning around the first of September
for as long as I can remember
my father gets up to make me . . . AWFUL WAFFLES!
I chew them politely, wash them down with a drink
wishing I could toss them into a sink
because the outsides are mushy, the insides are hard
I know that the batter is goat's milk and lard!

flavorful french toast with maple yogurt sauce

Ingredients
2 eggs
⅓ cup regular milk or soy
   milk flavored with chocolate, strawberry, or eggnog
½ teaspoon vanilla extract
1 tablespoon margarine
6 slices of whole grain bread

Directions
Beat eggs, milk and vanilla in a large shallow bowl. Melt the margarine in a large skillet over medium heat. Cut bread diagonally and dip the slices into the batter, covering both sides. Brown the bread on one side then flip to the other. Remove from skillet and top with maple yogurt sauce.

Maple Yogurt Sauce
Blend together ½ cup of low-fat or nonfat plain yogurt with 1 tablespoon of pure maple syrup. Add more syrup to suit taste.

applesauce pancakes

Ingredients
1 cup oatmeal (not instant)
2 cups buttermilk
2 tablespoons sugar
1 teaspoon baking soda
¾ cup flour
2 eggs
Natural applesauce

Directions
In a large bowl, soak the oatmeal in the buttermilk for about 15 minutes. Sift the sugar, soda and flour together and stir into the oat mixture. Beat in the eggs, mixing thoroughly, and let stand for 15 minutes. Heat the skillet over medium heat, and brush with oil. Using a ½ cup measure, pour out rounds and brown on both sides. Butter the cakes as they are made and keep warm. Put applesauce between two pancakes and cut into wedges. Yield: 4 servings.

pear plumps

Ingredients
4 firm, ripe pears
⅓ cup quick-cooking oatmeal
⅓ cup crushed, unsweetened pineapple
¼ teaspoon ground cinnamon
¼ teaspoon pineapple juice concentrate (optional)
1 cup apple cider
1 cup natural plain yogurt
¼ teaspoon almond extract

Directions
Preheat oven to 350ºF (180ºC). Remove the cores from the pears to ½ inch from the base. Set them upright in a baking dish. Mix together oatmeal, pineapple, cinnamon and juice concentrate and fill the inside of the pears. Pour the apple cider around the pears. Cover with foil and bake for 30 to 40 minutes. Mix the yogurt and almond extract with the apple cider remaining in the pan. Spoon over the warm pears before serving. Yield: 4 servings.

eggs bennie

Ingredients
6 eggs
6 slices boneless cooked ham
3 English muffins

Hollandaise Sauce
½ cup butter, melted
1 egg
½ teaspoon Dijon mustard
½ tablespoon lemon juice

Directions
Fill a medium saucepan with 2 to 3 inches of water. Bring water to a boil. Crack eggs into the water and boil until eggs are done to your liking. Toast English muffins, and cut into little pieces. Cut ham into little pieces. Make hollandaise sauce by putting ingredients into a blender and mixing for one minute. Place English muffin and ham pieces on plate, top with egg and hollandaise sauce. Yield: 6 servings.

hawaiian toast

Ingredients
4 eggs
8 ounces (225 g) crushed pineapple
¼ cup milk
1 tablespoon each:
Maple syrup, sour cream and sugar
8 slices of bread
4 tablespoons butter
Powdered sugar
Shredded, unsweetened coconut

Directions
In a blender, whirl eggs, pineapple, milk, syrup, sour cream, and sugar until smooth. Trim bread slices and place in a large shallow dish. Pour egg mixture over bread and turn bread to coat other side. Melt 1 tablespoon of butter in a frying pan or skillet over medium heat. Place 2 slices of bread in pan and cook until browned on both sides. Repeat with remaining slices of bread. Before serving, dust with powdered sugar and sprinkle with coconut. Yield: 8 servings.

egg and cheese soufflé

Ingredients
12 slices of bread, crusts removed
1 cup grated cheddar cheese
1 cup diced ham (optional)
6 eggs
1½ cups milk
¼ teaspoon salt
¼ teaspoon pepper

Directions
Grease a 9x13-inch pan. Place 6 of the bread slices in the bottom of the pan. Sprinkle the cheese and ham over the top of the bread. Arrange the remaining six pieces of bread over the top of the cheese (like a sandwich). Combine the eggs, milk, and salt, and pour them over the bread. Refrigerate at least 6 hours or overnight. Bake, uncovered, at 325°F (165°C) for 55 minutes. Take out of oven. Cover with foil and wait 5 minutes. Cut into squares and serve. Yield: 6 servings.

apple cheese omelet

Ingredients
2 large tart apples, peeled, cored and sliced
1 tablespoon lemon juice
⅛ teaspoon each ground nutmeg and cinnamon
2 tablespoons butter or margarine
6 eggs
2 tablespoons milk or water
1 cup shredded cheddar cheese

Directions
In a bowl, mix apples, lemon juice, nutmeg and cinnamon. Melt ½ the butter in a pan over medium heat. Add apple mixture and stir until apples begin to brown. Remove from heat. Beat eggs and water together. In a frying pan or skillet, melt the remaining butter over medium-high heat. Add the egg mixture and cook until omelet is set but still moist on top. Spoon half the apple mixture and ½ cup cheese down center of omelet. Fold over to cover apples. Gently lift omelet onto plate and cover with remaining apples and cheese. Yield: 6 servings.

muesli and yogurt

Ingredients

2 cups flaked grains—oats, millet, buckwheat, or bran
1 cup nuts and seeds—sliced almonds, walnut pieces, pine nuts,
   sunflower seeds
1 cup chopped dried fruits—raisins, apricots, dates, or apples
Plain yogurt sweetened with honey

Directions

Store grains, seeds and dried fruits in separate sealed jars for added
freshness. At breakfast time, stir spoonfuls of each into bowls of yogurt.
Yield: 8–12 servings.

anything can scramble

Ingredients

8 eggs
4 tablespoons milk
Any of the following ingredients,
chopped or sliced:

 Onion
 Potato
 Green pepper
 Cheese
 Tomato
 Bacon
 Ham
 Hot dogs

Directions

Mix eggs together with milk. Fry the vegetables in butter until cooked thoroughly. Then pour egg mixture into skillet and scramble everything together. Top with cheese or serve plain. Ingredients that do not need to be cooked can be added into the egg scramble last, with just enough time to warm them through. Yield: 4 servings.

blueberry breakfast cake

Ingredients
1 tablespoon butter
1¼ cup flour
1 tablespoon baking powder
½ teaspoon salt
1¼ cup sugar
⅓ cup butter, melted and cooled
3 tablespoons vanilla extract
3 eggs
3 cups fresh or frozen blueberries
¾ cup sour cream

Crumb Topping
¾ cup light brown sugar
½ cup butter cut into small pieces
1½ cups flour

Directions
Preheat oven to 350°F (180°C). With tablespoon of butter coat a 7x15 baking pan. Dust with flour. Refrigerate the pan. In large bowl, combine flour, baking powder, salt and sugar. Add the melted butter, vanilla, and eggs. Mix until well combined. Fold in the blueberries and sour cream. Pour batter into baking pan. In a separate bowl, combine brown sugar and butter pieces. Add flour and mix. Sprinkle evenly over cake batter. Bake 40 minutes or until a toothpick inserted in the center comes out clean. Yield: 12–15 servings.

stuffed tomatoes

Ingredients
4 large firm tomatoes
½ teaspoon salt
¼ teaspoon pepper
8 small eggs
4 teaspoons grated Parmesan cheese

Directions
Preheat oven to 350°F (180°C). Cut tomatoes in half crosswise. Scoop out the pulp from each, leaving a half-inch shell. Invert the tomatoes on paper towels to drain. Place tomato shells in a shallow pan cut side up. Break an egg into each tomato and sprinkle cheese on top. Bake for 20 minutes or until eggs are firm. Yield: 8 servings.

Mealtime Question: Ask, "If you could change anything about yourself, what would it be?"

aunt katie's coffee cake

Ingredients
1 cup butter or margarine
2 cups sugar
3 eggs
2 cups unbleached flour
1 teaspoon baking powder
½ teaspoon salt
8 ounces (225 g) sour cream or natural yogurt
1 teaspoon each vanilla, lemon and almond extract
½ cup brown sugar
4 teaspoons cinnamon
1 cup ground pecans

Directions
In a large bowl, cream butter and sugar for 8 minutes. Add the eggs, beating in between. Add flour, baking powder, and salt, alternating with the sour cream. Add extracts. Pour half of the batter into a greased and floured tube or bundt pan. In a separate bowl, mix the brown sugar, cinnamon, and pecans. Sprinkle half of the pecan mixture over the batter. Cover with remaining batter and the rest of the pecan mixture. Bake for 1 hour. Cool the cake in the pan for 5 minutes then transfer to a plate. Yield: 12–15 servings.

crepes surprise

Ingredients
2 cups unbleached flour
1 egg, beaten
2½ cups milk
¼ teaspoon salt
Cooking oil
Berries, coconut, raisins, banana, sliced apples, etc.

Directions
Place flour in a bowl and add egg, 2 cups milk, and salt. Beat with a wire whip until all lumps are gone. Gradually add remaining ½ cup milk to make a thin batter. Heat skillet to medium-high (350°F or 180°C). Melt 1 teaspoon of oil making sure it covers the bottom of the pan. Pour enough batter into pan to make a large circle. Sprinkle fruit on top and press down into the crepe. Cook a few more minutes, then flip over and cook the other side. Lift onto a warm plate and roll up like a jelly roll. Yield: 4–6 servings.

big apple pancake

Ingredients
½ cup unbleached flour
2 eggs
½ cup milk
¼ cup butter
1 apple, peeled and sliced
¼ cup sugar
2 teaspoons cinnamon

Directions
Preheat oven to 400°F (200°C). Mix together flour, eggs and milk and set aside. Melt butter in a skillet and cook apple over medium heat until soft. Add sugar and cinnamon. Pour liquid over the top of the cooked apple and cook in an oven for 20 minutes. Turn over onto a plate immediately, apple side up. Yield: 4 servings.

Note: This is also a tasty dessert topped with Cool Whip.

warm rice and blueberries

Ingredients
1 cup cooked long grain white rice
½ cup blueberries
¼ teaspoon nutmeg
3 teaspoons honey
½ cup hot milk

Directions
Spoon rice and blueberries into bowls. Sprinkle with honey and nutmeg.
Pour hot milk over top and serve. If using leftover rice, warm rice, milk,
and honey in a saucepan before adding blueberries. Yield: 2 servings.

puff baby

Ingredients
½ cup unbleached flour
2 eggs
½ cup milk
¼ cup butter
Powdered sugar
Lemon, cut into wedges

Directions
Preheat oven to 400°F (200°C). Mix flour, eggs, and milk together, leaving batter a bit lumpy. Melt butter in a 9 inch pie plate. Pour batter on top of butter. Bake for 20 minutes or until golden brown and puffy. Sift powdered sugar on top and squeeze lemon to desired amount. Serve immediately. Yield: 2 servings.

Note: You might want to double the recipe to make two 9-inch puffs.

stuffed french toast

Ingredients

1 package (8 ounces) cream cheese, softened
1½ teaspoons vanilla extract
1 teaspoon honey
1 or 2 sliced bananas (optional)
1 loaf soft French bread
4 eggs, beaten
1 cup milk
1 jar apricot or peach preserves

Directions

Beat the cream cheese, vanilla, and honey until creamy. Stir in the pecans and set aside. Cut the bread into 1½-inch thick slices. Cut a slit in each slice, creating a pocket. Fill each pocket with 1 to 2 tablespoons of the cheese mixture. Mix the eggs and milk together in a small bowl. Dip the pieces of bread in the egg and milk mixture before frying them on both sides in a frying pan over medium heat. Serve topped with a spoonful of preserves. Yield: 4–6 servings.

pigs in a blanket

Ingredients
2 eggs
2 cups unbleached flour
1½ cups milk
4 tablespoons melted butter or vegetable oil
1 tablespoon sugar
4 teaspoons baking powder
½ teaspoon salt
Breakfast sausages (2 per person)

Directions
Mix together eggs, flour, milk, butter, sugar, baking powder, and salt.
Make pancakes by pouring batter into a large frying pan in 5-inch circles.
Cook pancakes over medium heat until small holes form, then turn over
until brown. Fry sausages in a separate fry pan. Roll pancakes around
each sausage. Can be served with maple syrup.

fruits

Little green banana
so good for my health
sitting very proudly
on my kitchen shelf

Sunning by the window
feeling sweet and mellow
passing each day
without turning yellow

Little green banana
it was so nice to meet you
but now that we've met
I don't think I can eat you!

fruity banana split

Ingredients
4 bananas
2 cups cottage cheese
Large can of fruit cocktail

Directions
Cut each banana into 4 pieces. Put pieces into a bowl. Put ½ cup of cottage cheese on top of the bananas. Cover generously with the fruit cocktail. This is a nice play snack for kids to help make. Yield: 4 servings.

Note: Words are less important than the judgments that accompany them, according to Dorothy Carkille Briggs, teacher of parent education. She writes in her book, *Your Child's Self Esteem*, that the child's own judgment of herself emerges from the judgments of others and the more she likes her self-image, the higher her self-esteem (New York: Doubleday, 1975, p.19).

apple fritters

Ingredients
4 cooking apples, peeled and cored
1¼ cups unbleached flour
½ teaspoon baking powder
2 tablespoons sugar
2 eggs, separated
½ cup milk
Vegetable oil for cooking

Directions
Cut apples into small chunks. Sift together the flour, baking powder, and sugar. Beat egg yolks and milk together and stir into dry ingredients. Add apples. Beat egg whites until stiff and fold into the mixture. Heat ½ cup vegetable oil in a deep fry pan. Drop tablespoons of batter into hot oil and cook until golden brown on both sides. Serve warm, sprinkled with cinnamon sugar. Yield: 12 servings.

roast chicken with grapes

Ingredients
Roasting chicken
½ cup butter at room temperature
½ cup white wine or chicken broth
Parsley and thyme

Sauce
3 tablespoons butter
1 tablespoon flour
Juice from pan plus extra chicken stock
20 firm grapes

Directions
Preheat the oven to 400°F (200°C). Spread ¼ cup butter over the chicken and cover with foil. Mix ¼ cup butter with herbs and insert inside chicken. Place chicken in a small roasting dish and pour the wine on top. Re-cover with the foil. Roast chicken 1 to 1½ hours, removing from oven every 20 minutes to baste. Add a little extra wine or broth if chicken is drying up. When chicken is cooked, remove from pan and keep it warm. Make a roux sauce by frying 3 tablespoons butter in a pan, add the flour and cook until browned. Add the juice from the pan, adding extra chicken stock as required. Simmer 10 minutes. Just before serving, warm the prepared grapes in the sauce. Spoon grape sauce over the jointed chicken. Yield: 4–6 servings.

apple apricot compote

Ingredients
1 cup water
1 teaspoon freshly squeezed lemon or orange juice
¼ cup sugar
2 apples (Braeburn, Cortland, or Jonagold), peeled,
  cored and cut into cubes
8 fresh apricots, pitted and sliced

Directions
In a medium saucepan, combine the water, juice, and sugar over medium heat and cook for 3 to 4 minutes, swirling the saucepan until the sugar dissolves. Add the apples and cook for 6 to 8 minutes, until the apples are tender, but not soft. Add the apricots and cook an additional 2 minutes. Serve warm or cool with a garnish of mint or lemon peel. Yield: 4 servings.

fall fruit medley

Ingredients
1 can pineapple chunks
3 apples, cored and chopped
3 oranges, peeled and cut up
1 cup green grapes
1 cup red grapes
2 bananas, peeled and sliced
1 cup chopped nuts and raisins
½ cup each honey and plain yogurt

Directions
Drain pineapple and reserve juice for dressing. Place all the fruit in a large bowl and toss to mix. Arrange on bed of fall leaves which have been rinsed and patted dry. Make dressing by blending pineapple juice, honey, and yogurt. Pour over fruit before serving. Yield: 6 servings.

Note: Yogurt is natural and provides needed friendly bacteria for digestion. It is known by other names too. Kefir is from camel's milk and kumiss is from mare's milk. Most yogurt today is made from cow's milk, although originally it was from ewe's milk.

hot apple scrunch

Ingredients
4 cooking apples, cored, peeled and sliced
½ cup currants
¼ cup honey
1 teaspoon cinnamon
Juice of 1 lemon
½ cup apple juice

Topping
½ cup melted butter
2 teaspoons cinnamon
1 teaspoon vanilla
2 cups uncooked oatmeal

Directions
Preheat oven to 350°F (180°C). Mix all ingredients (except topping) and spoon into a greased baking dish. Add extra apple juice to barely cover apples. Combine topping ingredients and sprinkle over apples. Bake for 40 minutes or until crust is golden brown. Yield: 6 servings.

grilled bananas

Ingredients
2 bananas
Sprinkling of raisins
1 teaspoon brown sugar or honey
1 teaspoon lemon juice
Dash of orange juice
Natural yogurt or ice cream

Directions
Preheat the oven to 450°F (240°C). Peel the bananas and slice lengthwise. Lay in a heat-proof dish. Sprinkle the banana halves with raisins, lemon and orange juice, brown sugar, or honey. Cover with foil and bake for 5 to 10 minutes. At the end, remove the foil for a few minutes. Serve hot with yogurt or ice cream. Yield: 2 servings.

caramel apple chunks

Ingredients
5 medium apples
1 pound (500 g) caramels
2 tablespoons water

Directions
Wash, dry, and cut up the apples into bite-size pieces. Divide and place in individual bowls (6). In a small saucepan or in microwave oven, heat the caramels and water, stirring constantly. When melted and smooth, pour over the apples. Wait until cool before serving. Yield: 6 servings.

chocolate-dipped fruit

Ingredients

Bananas, strawberries, cantaloupe
½ pound semisweet white or dark chocolate
1 tablespoon solid vegetable shortening
Toothpicks or skewers

Directions

Wash strawberries and pat dry with paper towel, peel bananas, and cut cantaloupe into large chunks. In a double boiler over hot but not boiling water, melt chocolate and vegetable shortening, stirring carefully. Leave the bottom of the double boiler on the flame and take the top with the chocolate in it to your work surface. If the chocolate begins to harden, return to the heat. Stick a toothpick or skewer into each piece of fruit. Dip ⅔ of the fruit into the chocolate coating, letting the excess chocolate drip back into the pan. Chill fruit until chocolate is hardened. Yield: 12 fruit pieces.

Note: A good way to let the chocolate harden is to stick the toothpicks into a Styrofoam block covered with plastic wrap.

fairy-tale ambrosia

Ingredients
1 orange
½ cantaloupe
2 cups grapes
1 banana
½ cup shredded coconut
Orange juice

Directions
Peel orange, cantaloupe, and banana. Cut fruit into small pieces and add rinsed grapes. Arrange alternate layers of fruit and coconut, leaving some coconut for sprinkling on top. Pour a little orange juice over the fruit and chill before serving. Yield: 4 servings.

Note: Ambrosia means "the food of the gods and goddesses" and is used to describe foods that are delicious or fragrant.

apple and carrot soup

Ingredients

1 pound carrots, peeled and diced
1 onion, finely chopped
1 medium potato, peeled and diced
1 large apple, peeled, cored, and roughly chopped
1 ounce butter
1 ounce barley, rinsed in cold water
2 pints vegetable stock
1 tablespoon tomato puree

Directions

Melt the butter in a saucepan. Stir in the carrots, onion, and potato and cook gently for a few minutes, stirring to prevent sticking or browning. Stir in the apple, stock, and tomato puree. Bring to a boil and add the pot barley. Stir, reduce the heat to a simmer, cover, and cook for about 45 minutes to one hour, or until the barley is tender. Remove from the heat, allow to cool then blend with hand mixer or blender. Reheat before serving. Yield: 4–6 servings.

apple, spinach, and feta strudel

Ingredients
1 tablespoon olive oil
2 bunches spinach, washed and sliced
2 apples, grated
1 cup feta cheese, crumbled
1 teaspoon oregano
1 egg
Pinch of nutmeg
Black pepper
5 sheets phyllo pastry
¼ cup butter, melted

Directions
Preheat the oven to 350°F (180°C). Heat the oil in a pan and add the spinach and grated apples. Cook until dry. Place the mixture in a bowl and add the feta, oregano, egg, nutmeg, and pepper. Mix well. Place a sheet of phyllo pastry on a board and brush with melted butter. Place another sheet on top brushing with butter. Continue until all sheets have been used. Spread the filling over the pastry, leaving a half-inch edge all around. Fold the long edges in, then roll up to form a log. Brush lightly with butter and place on a greased baking sheet, folded edge down. Bake for 25 to 30 minutes, or until golden brown. Yield: 5 servings.

pot of gold salad with creamy pineapple dressing

Ingredients
1 can chunk pineapple
2 bananas, peeled
2 oranges, peeled
1 melon, peeled and balled
Lettuce leaves, bib or butter

Directions
Drain pineapple, saving juice for dressing. Slice bananas and dice oranges. Line 4 plates with lettuce leaves. Arrange fruit on lettuce. Top with Creamy Pineapple dressing. Yield: 4 servings.

Creamy Pineapple Dressing
Pour pineapple juice into blender. Add 2 tablespoons lemon juice, ½ cup cottage cheese and a pinch of salt. Blend until smooth.

Note: Children often don't eat oranges because they find them difficult to peel. Try soaking an orange in boiling water first. Cool under cold water and the skin will peel off more easily.

apple dumpling

Ingredients

2 cups unbleached flour
½ teaspoon salt
½ cup butter
1 cup grated cheddar cheese
6 tablespoons cold water
6 small apples, cored
2 tablespoons brown sugar
⅓ cup fines chopped pecans

Sauce
½ cup sugar
1 tablespoon corn flour
½ teaspoon nutmeg
Pinch salt
1 cup water
2 tablespoons lemon juice
1 teaspoon grated lemon peel
2 tablespoons butter

Directions

Preheat the oven to 350°F (180°C). Combine the flour and salt in a bowl, cut in the butter and stir in the cheese. Gradually add the water until it is absorbed. Gather the dough into a ball and roll out on a floured surface to form a rectangle. Cut into 5-inch squares. Place an apple upside down in the center of each square. Combine the sugar and pecans and fill the apple cavities with the mixture. Gather up the dough and pinch the seams to seal. Place on an ungreased baking sheet. If there is any reserve dough, have the child make leaves or other design with it and place on the top of the apples with milk to hold it. Prick with a fork and bake for 45 to 50 minutes or until light brown.

To make the sauce, combine all the ingredients except the lemon juice, peel, and butter. Heat together and cook for 3 to 4 minutes, stirring constantly. Remove from the heat and add the lemon juice, peel, and butter, stirring until the butter is melted. Serve warm over the dumplings.

apricot chicken breasts

Ingredients
4 chicken breasts, skinned and boned
1 cup dried apricots, finely chopped
Salt and ground pepper
1 egg
1 tablespoon oil
2 tablespoons orange juice
1 tablespoon butter
3 pears peeled, cored, and diced
1 tablespoon fresh ginger, cut into slivers
1 tablespoon brown sugar
1 tablespoon lemon juice

Directions
Using a sharp knife, make a pocket in each chicken breast. Combine the apricots, seasonings, and egg, and mix well. Divide the mixture into four and fill each pocket, securing with a toothpick. Heat the oil in a fry pan, and brown the chicken breasts. Add the orange juice, cover, and cook over low heat for 7 to 10 minutes, or until chicken is cooked through. Set the chicken breasts aside and keep warm. Heat the butter in the fry pan, add the pears and ginger, and cook for 5 minutes, stirring often. Add the brown sugar and the lemon juice, and cook a few minutes. Slice the chicken breasts to show the inside stuffing and serve with the pear and ginger mixture. Yield: 4 servings.

apple and grape salad

Ingredients

30 fresh grapes, washed and dried
2 red apples, sliced
1 cup low-fat yogurt
3 tablespoons sour cream
2 tablespoons honey, melted

Directions

Place the grapes in the freezer to get really cold for half an hour. Combine with the sliced apples in a bowl. Mix yogurt, sour cream and melted honey together and pour over the fruit. Yield: 4–5 servings.

sausage and fruit bake

Ingredients
6 sausages
1 tablespoon oil
2 onions, halved and cut in thin slices
1 cup orange juice
½ teaspoon ground ginger
1 apple, sliced into matchsticks
½ cup raisins
2 teaspoons cornstarch mixed with ¼ cup sherry or apple juice

Directions
Boil the sausages in plenty of water for 7 to 8 minutes. Drain and allow to cool, then slice in thin diagonals. Heat a skillet, add the oil, and cook the onions. Add the spices and the remaining ingredients, including the sliced sausages, and mix through. Season to taste, cover, and simmer for 10 minutes. Yield: 4 servings.

do-it-yourself

Marshmallow Meatloaf
Gravy with Cherries
Chocolate Potatoes
Broccoli and Berries
alone in the kitchen
busy as elves
cooking a dish
they created themselves.

maley milkshake

Ingredients
1 cup low-fat milk
3 scoops natural vanilla ice cream
2 teaspoons natural jam, carob powder, or chocolate sauce

Directions
Wash hands before starting. Get out ingredients. Put all ingredients into a blender and blend on medium-high speed for 2 to 3 minutes. Pour into glasses and enjoy. Yield: 3–4 servings.

Note: In *Literacy Begins at Birth*, (California Bill's Automotive, 1989) Dr. Marjorie Fields explains that taking time to read to your children almost assures that they will later love to read.

cinnamon toast

Ingredients
4 slices whole wheat bread
2 tablespoons butter or margarine
½ teaspoon cinnamon
3 tablespoons soft brown sugar

Directions
Wash hands before starting. Set all ingredients on table. Toast bread in toaster, 2 slices at a time. Mix cinnamon and brown sugar together. Remove toast from toaster and spread with margarine while it is still warm. Sprinkle cinnamon sugar on top. Cut into triangles and enjoy. Yield: 4 servings.

boiled eggs

Ingredients
Fresh eggs
Whole grain bread
Butter or natural jam

Directions
Wash hands before starting. Get out all ingredients. Put eggs in a medium-sized saucepan. Cover them with cold water. Bring water to boil over high heat. Reduce heat and simmer (barely boiling for desired time).

Soft eggs—3 minutes
Medium eggs—5 minutes
Hard-boiled eggs—20 minutes

Remove from heat. Cover eggs with cold water. Put toast in toaster, either peel egg or crack in half with spoon. Eat with toast that has been cut into fingers.

homemade cheese

Ingredients
1 quart (1 liter) milk
1 lemon
Strainer (fine)
Cheesecloth

Directions
Wash hands before starting. Place all ingredients on a table or bench.
Pour milk into a saucepan and heat until it barely boils. Be careful to not
let it boil over. Add the juice of the lemon. Milk will separate into curds
and whey. Pour through the strainer so that curds are left behind. Empty
the curds onto a square of cheesecloth and bring corners together. Form
a tight ball by twisting and squeezing out remaining moisture. Chill.
Remove from cheesecloth and spread on bread or crackers.

raspberry passion fruit swirls

Ingredients
2 cups raspberries
2 passion fruit
1½ cups plain yogurt or crème fraiche
2 tablespoons sugar
Raspberries and fresh mint leaves for decoration

Directions
Wash hands before starting. Mash the raspberries in a small bowl until the juice runs. Scoop out the passion fruit pulp into another bowl and mix in the yogurt or crème fraiche. Sweeten with sugar and mix well. Place alternate spoonfuls of the raspberry pulp and the passion fruit mixture in stemmed or parfait glasses. Stir slightly to create a swirled effect. Decorate each glass with a raspberry and sprig of mint leaves. Serve chilled. Yield: 4 servings.

Hint: Other delicious fruit combinations would be ripe peaches or straw-berries with mango or blueberries. Drizzle the top with honey if desired.

blueberry crepes

Ingredients
1 cup unbleached flour
1 egg beaten
1¼ cups milk
Pinch of salt
1 cup fresh blueberries
Butter or margarine
Powdered sugar

Directions
Wash hands before starting. Place all ingredients on table or bench. Put flour and salt into a bowl. Add egg and half of the milk and mix well. Stir in remaining milk.

Put 1 tablespoon of butter in a frying pan over medium heat. Drop crepe batter by large tablespoons into pan. Drop several blueberries onto each crepe. Turn crepe over when the edges start to bubble. Lift onto a plate and dust with powdered sugar. Serve warm. Yield: 4 servings.

egg nests

Ingredients
1¼ pounds ground meat
½ cup bread crumbs
4 tablespoons grated Parmesan cheese
4 mashed potatoes
8 eggs
7 tablespoons melted butter
Salt and pepper to taste

Directions
Wash hands before starting. Get out all ingredients. Preheat oven to 350°F (180°C). Mix meat, bread crumbs, cheese, mashed potatoes, salt, and pepper in a bowl. Make nests by forming 8 balls out of meat. Flatten and make a depression in center. Place in buttered ovenproof dish and cook for 30 minutes. Remove from oven, crack egg in nest, sprinkle with salt, and return to oven for 12 minutes. Yield: 8 servings.

crackers

Ingredients

2 cups unbleached white flour
2 cups whole wheat flour
1 cup unsweetened fruit juice
⅓ cup vegetable oil
Pinch of salt

Directions

Wash hands before starting. Get out all ingredients. Preheat oven to 375°F (190°C). In mixing bowl, combine 1 cup white flour, 1 cup wheat flour, fruit juice, salt, and oil until smooth. Add the rest of the flour slowly until a soft dough is formed.

Roll half of the dough at a time very thin on a floured surface. Cut with cookie cutters and place on nonstick baking sheets. Bake 8 to 10 minutes until the edges begin to brown.

yummy parfaits

Ingredients
4 cups fresh fruit
1 cup whipped topping
2 small boxes instant pudding
Garnishes: raisins, coconut, nuts, carob chips, etc.

Directions
Wash hands before starting. Get out all ingredients. Get out clear glasses of any kind (dessert, wine, or water). Make pudding according to box directions. Prepare fruit, wash, and cut into small pieces. Put garnishes in readily available piles. Begin layering pudding, fruit, and garnishes in any way you like. Be creative! Top with whipped topping. Serve to Mom or Dad! Yield: 6–8 servings.

grilled peanut butter sandwich

Ingredients
8 slices whole grain bread
Natural peanut butter
Margarine or butter
Natural fruit jam

Directions
Wash hands before starting. Spread margarine on all slices of bread. Place the bread, margarine side down, on a clean surface. Spread peanut butter on 4 of the slices and jam on the other 4. Put peanut butter and jam slices together. Place in frying pan over medium heat, butter side down. Cook until golden brown on both sides or remove when jam or peanut butter oozes out.

berries and cream

Ingredients
1 pint strawberries, raspberries, or blueberries
1 cup plain natural yogurt
6 tablespoons brown sugar

Directions
Wash hands before starting. Get all ingredients out. Clean fruit, pull off green tops, and cut into small pieces (if using strawberries). Put fruit into a pretty bowl. Put yogurt on top of the fruit and mix. Sprinkle brown sugar on top. Yield: 4 servings.

eggs in a bun

Ingredients
4 hamburger buns
Soft butter or margarine
4 eggs
Salt and pepper
4 slices of cheese

Directions
Wash hands before starting. Preheat oven to 350°F (180°C). Place all ingredients on a table with a round cookie cutter. Using the cookie cutter, cut a hole in the top half of the buns. Remove the bun circles with a fork. Butter the insides of the buns and place them on a baking sheet. Break an egg into each hole and lightly sprinkle with salt and pepper. Bake in oven for 20 minutes then place cheese slice over the bun. Bake 5 more minutes or until cheese is melted. Serve warm.

creamy fettuccine

Ingredients
½ stick of soft butter
¼ cup cream or half and half
½ cup grated Parmesan cheese
4 quarts water
1 teaspoon salt
12 ounces (340 g) fettuccine or egg noodles

Directions
Wash hands before starting. Place all ingredients on table or bench. Warm the butter and cream together on the stovetop or in a microwave oven. In a large saucepan, boil the water and add salt. Add the noodles and stir gently. Cook according to directions uncovered for 8 to 10 minutes. Drain. Put noodles in a large serving bowl and stir in the cheese mixture until blended. Pour warm cream and butter mixture over the top. Before serving, garnish with slices of fresh vegetables. Yield 4 servings.

fish in a blanket

Ingredients
1 pound (900 g) sole
6 slices boiled ham
1 lemon
6 teaspoons Parmesan cheese
3 tablespoons olive oil
Aluminum foil cut into 12-inch sections

Directions
Wash hands before starting. Get out all ingredients. Read through recipe. Preheat oven to 400°F (200°C).

Cut fish into 6 pieces. Place each ham slice in the center of the foil squares. Place one fish fillet on top of each ham slice. Brush olive oil on top of fish. Squeeze lemon juice on each fish. Sprinkle one teaspoon Parmesan cheese over fish. Roll up ham with fish inside it. Wrap each fish roll in tinfoil and seal it tight. Put rolls in a pan and bake for 35 minutes. Yield: 6 servings.

layered M&M bars

Ingredients
18 whole graham crackers
1 cup (2 sticks) margarine
1 cup brown sugar
½ teaspoon vanilla extract
1 six ounce packet white chocolate chips
1 cup chopped M&M's

Directions
Wash hands before starting. Place all ingredients on table or bench. Preheat oven to 350°F (180°C). Lightly butter a cookie sheet. Arrange graham crackers side by side on cookie sheet. Melt butter and sugar in a saucepan over medium heat. Add vanilla and stir. Increase heat and boil for 1 minute. Pour mixture over crackers and top with chopped M&Ms. Bake until topping bubbles and turns brown. Remove from heat and immediately sprinkle white chocolate chips over cookies. Cool, then cut along cracker edges to separate before serving.

green eggs and ham

Ingredients

4 eggs
4 tablespoons milk
1 tablespoon melted butter
½ teaspoon salt
Pepper to taste
4 drops green food coloring
4 small thick slices cooked ham

Directions

Break the eggs into a large bowl. You may wish to show your child how to break an egg with the first one. Add the milk and food coloring and sprinkle with the salt and a little pepper. Beat the eggs with a fork or whisk until barely blended. Heat a skillet over medium heat and brush the bottom and sides with butter. Pour in the egg mixture and as it begins to set, stir gently with a spatula. Cook the egg mixture until set, but still moist, stirring so that the mixture does not stick to the skillet. Remove from the heat. Arrange the ham slices on warmed plates. Pile the eggs onto the ham, dividing the mixture into fourths. Serve immediately with buttered toast or muffin halves. Yield: 4 servings

peanut butter

Peanut Butter Brownies
Peanut Butter Soup
Peanut Butter Milkshake
The favorite of my group.

Munchy . . . Crunchy . . .
Sticky . . . Chewy . . .
Hunky . . . Chunky . . .
Creamy . . . Gooey . . .

Nutritiously delicious
Each and every bite
Hooray for peanut butter
Morning, noon, or night!

peanut butter croquettes

Ingredients

2 pounds potatoes, peeled and quartered
3 tablespoons vegetable oil
1 large onion, peeled and chopped
3 carrots, peeled and coarsely grated
1 small zucchini, scrubbed and sliced
1 cup mushrooms, chopped
1 tablespoon dried mixed herbs
4 oz grated cheddar cheese
½ cup crunchy peanut butter
2 eggs, beaten
½ cup dry breadcrumbs
3 tablespoons grated parmesan cheese

Directions

Bring potatoes to boil in a saucepan of water and simmer for 20 minutes, or until tender. Drain and mash thoroughly. In a fry-pan, heat the oil and cook onions and carrots over a low heat for 5 minutes. Add the zucchini and mushrooms and cook for 5 minutes more. Put the potatoes in a large bowl and stir in the vegetables, dried herbs, cheese, and peanut butter. When cool enough to handle, stir in 1/2 the beaten eggs. Divide mixture into 12 pieces and shape into fingers or rounds. Chill until firm. Put the remaining beaten egg in a shallow bowl. Mix the breadcrumbs and Parmesan cheese into a second shallow bowl. Dip each croquette into egg and then breadcrumbs until evenly coated. Heat oil in a deep fry-pan or deep-fat frier. Fry the croquettes for 3–5 minutes until golden brown. Drain well on paper towels and serve warm with a green salad. Yield: 6–12.

peanut butter oatmeal

Ingredients
4 cups low-fat milk
2 cups rolled oats (not instant)
¼ cup chopped dried fruit (optional)
4 teaspoons natural peanut butter
4 teaspoons honey

Directions
Heat milk to almost boiling, and then slowly add oats and fruit, stirring constantly. Reduce heat and cook about 10 minutes or until thickened. Pour into bowls and add one teaspoon of peanut butter and one teaspoon of honey to each. Stir well. Yield: 4 servings.

Note: Dr. George Washington Carver spent 50 years studying the peanut plant. He discovered over 300 uses for peanuts—including soap, ink, dye, floor coverings, cosmetic cream, and peanut butter.

pb and pineapple sandwiches

Ingredients
⅔ cup natural chunky peanut butter
1½ ounces (40 g) cream cheese, softened
½ cup drained crushed pineapple
¼ cup shredded carrot
8 slices whole grain sandwich bread

Directions
In a small bowl, stir together the peanut butter and softened cream cheese. Stir in the pineapple and carrot. Spread the mixture on four slices of the bread and top with the remaining slices. Yield: 4 servings.

Note: Given enough time and freedom of choice, children will develop a taste for many foods . . . but children, especially younger ones, are traditionalists. They are reluctant to try new things. From *The Practical Parent* by Genevieve Painter and Raymond Corsini (New York: Simon & Schuster, 1984, p. 56).

smoothie

Ingredients
½ cup peanut butter
¼ cup nonfat dry milk powder
½ cup ice cream or frozen yogurt
¼ teaspoon vanilla extract
1 large banana

Directions
Combine all ingredients in a blender and mix on medium for 30 seconds until smooth. Pour into small paper cups and chill for at least an hour. Serve cold. Yield: 4 servings.

peanutty popcorn balls

Ingredients
2 cups sugar
⅔ cup apple cider
⅔ cup real maple syrup
½ cup butter
1½ teaspoons salt
½ teaspoon vanilla
18 cups popped corn
1 cup salted peanuts
1 cup raisins

Directions
Combine sugar, apple cider, syrup, butter, and salt in a saucepan. Bring to a boil, stirring occasionally. Cook until the mixture reaches a soft ball stage. Add vanilla. Pour mixture over the popped corn, peanuts and raisins. Mix well. Once cool enough, with buttered hands, shape into balls and place on waxed paper. Yield: 12 balls.

pb chip muffins

Ingredients

2 eggs
¼ cup mashed banana
¼ cup natural peanut butter
⅓ cup vegetable oil
1 cup milk
¼ cup apple juice concentrate, thawed
¼ cup nonfat dry milk powder
2¼ cups unbleached white flour
1½ teaspoons baking powder
1 teaspoon baking soda
1 cup carob or chocolate chips

Directions

Preheat oven to 350°F (180°C). In a medium bowl, mix together the first 7 ingredients until creamy. Stir in the flour, baking powder, and baking soda. Add the carob chips. Fill muffin cups ⅔ full and bake 15 to 17 minutes. Yield: 12 servings.

vegetable peanut dip

Ingredients
½ cup natural peanut butter
½ cup plain low-fat yogurt
2 tablespoons maple syrup
Raw carrot sticks
Celery stalks
Fruit slices
Breadsticks and pretzel twigs

Directions
Blend the peanut butter (at room temperature), yogurt, and maple syrup together until smooth. Wash, peel, cut, and arrange dipping foods on a plate. Dip the prepared foods into the peanut mixture and enjoy. Yield: 2–6 servings.

pineapple pasta

Ingredients
12 ounces (350 g) fettuccine or egg noodles
¼ cup natural peanut butter (with no sugar added)
4 tablespoons milk
1 tablespoons salt
¼ cup crushed pineapple, drained

Directions
Bring water to boiling in a large pot. Cream the peanut butter, milk, salt, and pineapple in a bowl. Boil the noodles and stir gently. Cook uncovered for 8 minutes. Drain. Add the noodles to the peanut butter mixture. Stir until the noodles are covered. Yum! Yield: 6 servings.

Game: Instead of putting dinner on your child's plate, try putting a treasure map there that will lead her to her dinner.

peanut butter granola

Ingredients

3 cups rolled oats
1 cup coconut
½ cup sunflower seeds
½ cup toasted wheat germ
⅔ cup peanut butter
½ cup honey
¼ cup brown sugar
2 tablespoons vegetable cooking oil
½ cup raisins

Directions

Preheat oven to 300°F (150°C). Mix together the oats, coconut, seeds, and wheat germ. In a small saucepan, combine the peanut butter, corn honey, brown sugar, and oil. Cook and stir over medium heat until smooth. Pour over the oats mixture and stir until blended. Spread mixture in a baking pan. Bake 40 minutes, stirring every 10 minutes to prevent burning. Remove from oven and add raisins. Cool before serving. Yield: 12 servings.

Note: Whole nuts and seeds are recommended for children over 3 years.

no-bake nutty fruit drops

Ingredients

1½ cups natural peanut butter
1 cup (20) dried apricots
¼ cup honey
1 cup shredded coconut

Directions

Cut apricots into small pieces with kitchen scissors. Mix peanut butter and honey in a bowl. Stir in the apricots. Drop by teaspoons into coconut and roll until coated. Shape into balls. Place onto waxed paper and chill until firm. Yield: 24 drops.

Note: To avoid sticky fingers, place the coconut in a plastic bag. Drop balls into bag and shake gently until evenly covered.

lunch boxes

My lunch was packed
in a minute
Now I can't remember
what was in it.

An apple? Some carrots?
A muffin with jam?
An oatmeal cookie?
A sandwich with ham?

We eat in one hour
I can't wait to munch
on whatever it was
That I packed in my lunch!

cheddar cheese cookies

Ingredients
¾ cup flour
⅔ cup butter
⅓ cup firmly packed brown sugar
1 teaspoon vanilla
1 egg
½ teaspoon cinnamon
½ teaspoon baking powder
½ teaspoon salt
1½ cups oatmeal
1 cup shredded cheddar cheese
¾ cup raisins
1 cup apple, peeled and chopped

Directions
Preheat oven to 375°F (190°C). Combine flour, margarine, sugar, vanilla, egg, cinnamon, baking powder, and salt. Mix well. Add oatmeal, cheese, and raisins. Mix well. Stir in apple. Drop by tablespoons onto ungreased cookie sheet. Bake 15 minutes or until golden brown. Yield: 24 cookies.

tiny tuna souffles

Ingredients

7 ounces (200 g) tuna, packed in water
6 tablespoons plain yogurt
¼ apple, chopped
1 tablespoon lemon juice
1 tablespoon honey
1 teaspoon soy or tamari sauce
½ teaspoon mustard
4 tablespoons grated cheese
1 cup cooked brown rice
2 egg whites

Directions

Preheat oven to 375°F (180°C). Grease 2 muffin pans. In a large bowl, combine all ingredients except egg whites. Blend well. In another bowl, beat the egg whites until stiff peaks form. Fold egg whites into tuna mixture. Fill each muffin cup with tuna mixture until level with sides. Bake 45 minutes or until a toothpick comes out clean. Serve warm or cold. Yield: 12 servings.

baked bread sandwiches

Ingredients

Frozen loaf of white or wheat bread
  (the kind that has to rise)
Flour
Garlic salt
⅓ pound hard salami, thinly sliced
¼ pound mortadella, thinly sliced
⅓ pound ham, thinly sliced
⅓ pound Swiss cheese, thinly sliced
⅓ pound provolone cheese, thinly sliced
2 egg yolks, beaten

Directions

Thaw bread and let it rise, covered, in a warm spot for one hour. Punch down and knead with a small amount of flour. On floured surface, roll dough out into a 12 x 16 inch rectangle. Sprinkle with garlic salt. Tear the meat into bite-sized pieces and layer over the bread. Tear cheese into bite-sized pieces and layer over meat. Starting at the long end, roll up tightly in jelly roll fashion. Pinch ends together tightly and curve roll to form a crescent. Brush with beaten egg yolk. Place on cookie sheet and let rest 20 minutes. Bake at 375°F (190°C) for 25 to 30 minutes or until golden brown. Let rest a few minutes before thinly slicing. Yield: 8–12 servings. This is good to take along on a picnic and cut when you get there!

adventure chili

Ingredients
Favorite chili (from can or homemade)
Chopped onions
4 hot dogs
String
Thermos

Directions
Fill the thermos with hot chili and chopped onions. Then tie thread around cooked hot dogs and push them down into the chili. Leave the strings out when putting the lid on. Send along a bag of buns and napkins.

vegetable flat bread

Ingredients

1 cup carrots, washed, peeled, and grated
1 cup zucchini, washed, peeled, and grated
8 tablespoons grated Parmesan cheese
2 eggs, beaten
¼ cup olive oil
2 tablespoons chopped parsley
1 teaspoon oregano
1 tablespoon soy sauce

Directions

Preheat oven to 350°F (180°C). Place all of the ingredients in a large bowl and stir well. Grease a 9-inch square pan. Spread the mixture into the pan and bake for 20 to 25 minutes, until light brown. Cut when cool and pack for that special picnic, car trip, or lunch box. Yield: 12 servings.

potato cheese saucers

Ingredients
1 cup unbleached flour
¼ teaspoon salt
3 teaspoons baking powder
¼ cup butter or margarine
1 cup mashed potatoes
1 tablespoon milk beaten with 1 egg
8–12 cheese slices
Mustard (optional)

Directions
Preheat oven to 425°F (220°C). Sift flour, salt, and baking powder into a bowl. Cut or rub in the butter until the mixture becomes crumbly. Stir in potatoes. Add milk and egg mixture and stir into a soft, but not sticky, dough. Knead lightly on a floured surface then roll out to half-inch thickness. Using a cookie cutter, cut dough and place shapes on a greased cookie sheet. Bake for 12 to 15 minutes. Cool slightly and carefully slice each shape in half horizontally. Place cheese slice and mustard in between each half. Serve warm. Yield: 8–12 servings.

naturally soft pretzels

Ingredients
1 teaspoon salt
1 tablespoon active dry yeast
1 cup hot water
⅓ cup instant milk powder
¼ cup unsaturated vegetable oil
2 tablespoons honey
1½ cups flour
1 teaspoon baking soda
½ cup natural yogurt
2 cups flour (1 cup could be wheat flour)

Directions
In a large bowl, mix the first 7 ingredients very well. Cover with a clean, damp towel and set in a warm place to rise for 1 hour. Remove mixture from warm place and stir. Add the baking soda, yogurt, and the additional flour. Set aside until well-risen (about 3 hours). Knead down. Divide the dough into 10 equal pieces. Roll a piece into a long snake, about 20 inches by ½ inch, and then twist into an overhand knot or pretzel shape. Repeat until all pretzels are twisted. Simmer a few inches of water in the bottom of a wide pot. Place raw pretzels into the barely simmering water for a few seconds. Drain, then lay on a greased baking sheet. Sprinkle tops of pretzels with optional coatings: poppy seeds, Parmesan cheese, salt, etc. Starting in a cold oven, bake at 375°F (190°C) for 20 to 30 minutes, until brown. Yield: 12 pretzels.

bran apple bars

Ingredients
1 cup whole bran cereal
½ cup skim or low-fat milk
1 cup unbleached flour
1 teaspoon baking powder
½ teaspoon ground cinnamon
¼ teaspoon ground nutmeg
⅓ cup butter or margarine
½ cup brown sugar
2 egg whites
1 cup apple, peeled and chopped

Directions
Preheat oven to 350°F (180°C). Grease a 9x9-inch baking pan. Soak bran in milk until milk is absorbed. Mix dry ingredients thoroughly. In a large bowl, beat butter and sugar until creamy. Add egg whites, beating well. Stir in the chopped apple and bran mixture. Add dry ingredients. Mix well. Pour into pan. Bake 30 minutes or until a toothpick comes out clean. Cool before cutting into 16 bars. Yield: 16 servings.

cheese and whatever quiche

Ingredients
9-inch pie shell
1 tomato, squeezed, seeded
  and chopped (optional)
1 teaspoon salt
¾ cup grated Swiss cheese
1 cup half and half
3 large eggs
Optional ingredients:
Corn, peas, bacon bits, chopped onion

Directions
Preheat oven to 375°F (190°C). Sprinkle cheese, tomato, and optional ingredients on bottom of pie crust. Mix eggs, cream, and salt together. Pour over cheese and tomatoes. Bake 45 minutes or until center is firm and top browned and puffed. Wrap up and put in tomorrow's lunch, or eat warm. Yield: 8 servings.

Activity: Give your child a large piece of white butcher paper. Have them trace their plate, glass, fork, spoon, etc. Now let them eat their meal on the imaginary place setting.

grandma's granola

Ingredients

2½ cups uncooked oats (not "instant" oats)
½ cup coconut
½ cup almonds or seeds
   (omit for children under 3)
½ cup bran or Grape-Nuts (optional)
½ cup butter or margarine
½ cup honey
½ cup raisins or chopped dates

Directions

Mix together oats, coconut, almonds, and bran. Melt butter and honey and stir into dry ingredients. Spread evenly on a cookie tray. Bake at 300°F (150°C) for 20 minutes or until golden brown, stirring often. Stir in raisins. Cool before storing in an airtight jar or container. Yield: 12 servings.

Note: Sometimes honey becomes crystallized if it is stored for a long time. Set in hot water or briefly microwave to return it to its liquid state.

cheesy chocolate cupcakes

Ingredients
1½ cups unbleached flour
1 cup sugar
¼ cup cocoa or carob powder
1 teaspoon baking soda
½ cup oil
1 teaspoon vinegar
1 teaspoon vanilla
1 cup water
8 ounces (225 g) cream cheese
1 egg
⅓ cup sugar
Dash salt

Directions
Preheat oven to 350°F (180°C). Place muffin cups in muffin tin. Combine first 8 ingredients and beat well. Fill tins ½ full with chocolate mixture. Combine cheese, egg, and sugar in a small bowl and beat well. Drop 1 tablespoon of cheese mixture in each cupcake. Bake for 20 minutes. Yield: 12–15 cupcakes.

breadsticks

Ingredients
4 cups wheat, rye, or unbleached white flour
1 package dried yeast
½ teaspoon salt
3 tablespoons vegetable oil
1¼ cups milk

Directions
Sprinkle yeast on 3 tablespoons warm water and let sit until foamy. Place 3 cups flour and salt in a large bowl. Add yeast mixture, oil, and milk. Stir until blended. Add remaining flour until a soft dough forms. Knead on a floured surface until smooth and elastic (break off some pieces and let little hands knead also!). Return dough to bowl and let rise, covered, in a warm place for 1½ hours. Preheat oven to 450°F (230°C). Divide the dough into 32 pieces. With floured hands, roll each piece into a thin stick, 10 inches (25 cm) long. Place sticks on a lightly greased baking sheet. Cook for 15 minutes or until light brown. Yield: 32 servings.

Note: Breadsticks can be rolled in seeds, grains, or Parmesan cheese before baking. Brush with melted butter or beaten egg first.

spinach squares

Ingredients

2 eggs, beaten
1 cup milk
1 pound grated jack cheese
1 cup margarine, melted
1 cup flour
1 teaspoon garlic salt
1 teaspoon baking powder
⅓ cup Parmesan cheese
10 ounce package frozen spinach,
  chopped, thawed, and drained
Paprika
Parmesan cheese

Directions

Mix first 9 ingredients in order given. Spread them into a greased 15x10-inch jelly roll pan. Sprinkle with cheese and paprika. Bake at 425°F (220°C) for 15 to 20 minutes. Let stand for 5 minutes before slicing into squares. Yield: 8–10 servings.

oven-fried chicken

Ingredients
2½ pounds (1 kg) skinless chicken pieces
½ cup unbleached flour
2 eggs, beaten
½ teaspoon salt
½ teaspoon paprika
½ teaspoon onion salt (optional)
1 tablespoon lemon juice
1 tablespoon honey
¼ cup margarine
1 cup Italian seasoned bread crumbs

Directions
Preheat oven to 350°F (180°C). Place the flour and chicken pieces in a plastic bag and shake well. Beat together the eggs, salt, paprika, onion salt, lemon juice, and honey. Melt the margarine in a 9x13-inch baking pan. Pour the crumbs into a shallow container. Dip the floured chicken in the egg mixture and then in the crumbs turning to coat evenly, one piece at a time. Arrange coated chicken in the baking pan. Bake for 45 minutes or until fork tender. Turn chicken once during baking. Serve warm with fresh vegetables or cool and pack for a picnic. Yield: 6–8 servings.

rg trail mix

Ingredients
2 cups chocolate or carob chips
2 cups raisins
2 cups peanuts

Directions
Place ingredients in a large bowl and stir until mixed. Put in airtight container or sealed plastic bags and be prepared for an outing! Also add dried cranberries or almonds, if desired.

Activity: As you eat your picnic, lie on your backs and look at the clouds. Imagine what they could be.

crepe club sandwiches

Ingredients
1 cup unbleached flour
¼ teaspoon salt
2 eggs, beaten
1 cup skim or low-fat milk
Oil for cooking
12 thin slices ham or turkey
½ cup light cream cheese
2 medium tomatoes, thinly sliced

Directions
To make crepes, place flour and salt in a bowl and add the eggs, beating until blended. Gradually add the milk, beating constantly to form a smooth batter. Brush some oil onto a shallow nonstick pan and place over medium heat. Pour in 2–3 tablespoons of batter and swirl it around to make a thin pancake. Cook 1 minute or until pale brown and then turn over. Cook 1 more minute. Repeat until there are 6 crepes. Lay a crepe on a plate and place a slice of meat on it. Add another crepe, then a layer of cream cheese, another crepe, and then slices of tomato. Repeat with another 6 crepes and fillings. Chill for an hour and then cut each stack into wedges. Yield 6 servings.

lunch box mini meals

Ingredients

Honey-and-mustard-coated chicken strips
Couscous with cooked diced vegetables
Chopped hard-boiled eggs with macaroni and cheese
Bagel with cream cheese and fresh fruit slices
Pasta salad with shrimp and peas
Hummus with bagel rounds
Cottage cheese and pineapple
Cream cheese dip with smoked salmon
Pita bread, hummus, and cucumber slices
Carrot, zucchini, and celery sticks with peanut butter
Ham cubes, sweet pickle, and Wheat Thins
Citrus salad—orange, pink grapefruit, tangerine
Cubed turkey or chicken, sweet corn and red pepper salad with vinaigrette
Shredded carrot and raisin salad
Soup in small wide-mouthed flask

Directions

Healthy and interesting packed lunches are easy to prepare as long as parents have a checklist of options and do some advanced planning. Stock up and cook foods which can double as lunches the next day or can be stored in the freezer in small portion sizes. Ideally, a nutritionally balanced lunch box will include items from the main food groups: fruits and vegetables, grains and cereals, proteins, calcium-rich foods, and a drink.

salads

Olives, peppers, spinach greens
can be mixed with kidney beans,
tuna, crab or large sized prawns,
blended in with chopped pecans,
bits of apple, bits of pear
toss it high into the air
use a platter or a mold
serve it warm or serve it cold
top it with a fresh squeezed lime
SUPER SALADS every time!

rice salad

Ingredients

1 cup long grain rice
Peanut or vegetable oil
1 tablespoon honey
Pinch of dry mustard
2 tablespoons white wine vinegar
2 teaspoons poppy seeds
1 large navel orange, peeled and sectioned
8 ounces (225 g) pineapple cubes, drained
½ cup sliced strawberries

Directions

Cook rice following package directions. Transfer while still warm to a large bowl. Add 1 tablespoon of oil and toss lightly. Cool. In a bowl, combine honey, mustard, salt to taste, and vinegar. Beat until honey is dissolved. Gradually beat or blend in ¼ cup of oil. Add poppy seeds and pour over rice. Add orange, pineapple, and sliced strawberries. Toss lightly and serve. Yield: 4 servings.

german hot potato salad

Ingredients

5 or 6 medium potatoes
4 slices lean bacon
¼ cup finely chopped onion
1 tablespoon flour
1 teaspoon dry mustard
½ teaspoon salt
1 tablespoon sugar
½ cup water
1 egg, beaten
¼ cup vinegar

Directions

Scrub potatoes and cook in boiling water until tender. Drain. Hold potatoes under cold water and peel off skins. Slice into half-inch rounds and place in serving dish. Keep warm. Cook bacon in a skillet until crisp. Drain and chop into small pieces. Remove all but 2 tablespoons of bacon fat and stir in onion. Cook until golden brown. Blend in flour, mustard, salt, and sugar. When smooth, stir in water and cook for 2 minutes, stirring constantly. Stir 2 tablespoons of hot mixture into eggs and add remaining hot mixture and vinegar. Pour mixture over still warm potatoes. Sprinkle with bacon bits. Yield: 8 servings.

mandarin orange salad

Ingredients
½ cup sliced almonds
3 tablespoons honey
½ head iceberg lettuce
½ head romaine lettuce
1 cup chopped celery
2 green onions, sliced thin
11 ounce can mandarin oranges
1 cup chopped cooked chicken (optional)

Dressing
Mix together:
¼ cup vegetable oil
2 tablespoons chopped parsley
2 tablespoons honey
2 tablespoons vinegar
¼ teaspoon salt

Directions
In a small pan, cook almonds and honey, stirring until almonds are coated. Let cool. Shred lettuces and mix with celery and green onions. Just before serving, add almonds, chicken, and drained oranges to lettuce. Toss with the dressing. Yield: 6 servings.

fruity fall salad

Ingredients
3 ounce (74 g) packet lime Jell-O
½ cup mayonnaise
2 tablespoons lemon juice
¼ teaspoon salt
1 cup chopped apples
¾ cup seedless grapes
2 kiwi fruits, peeled and sliced

Directions
Dissolve the Jell-O in 1 cup of boiling water. Add ½ cup of cold water, mayonnaise, lemon juice, and salt. Blend well with a rotary beater or electric mixer. Pour into a freezer tray and quick chill for about 15 minutes. Turn chilled mixture into a bowl and beat again for about 3 minutes. Fold in the fruit. Pour into mold. Chill until jelled. Yield: 4 servings.

Note: This salad can be set in a fancy mold or in a Pyrex dish. Before serving, briefly set in hot water and then invert salad onto a serving dish. You and your child can gather fall leaves together and arrange them around the serving dish for a seasonal appearance.

cashew chicken surprise

Ingredients
8 ounces (450 g) uncooked shell macaroni
5 cups cooked, cubed chicken
1 cup celery
8 ounces (450 g) green peas, thawed
1 cup prepared buttermilk (Ranch) dressing
½ cup whole cashews
Lettuce leaves, rinsed

Directions
Cook macaroni as directed on package. Drain and rinse. Place macaroni, chicken, celery, and peas in a salad bowl. Pour dressing over top and blend all ingredients. Chill until serving time. Sprinkle cashews on top and serve on top of lettuce leaves. Yield: 6 servings.

tuna flowers

Ingredients
1 cup tuna packed in water, drained
½ cup diced celery
2 tablespoons lemon juice
¼ cup light mayonnaise
2 avocados, halved
2 tomatoes, sliced and peeled

Directions
Put tuna, celery, lemon juice and mayonnaise in a bowl and mix. Take seed out of avocado and place tuna salad in the center of avocado. Place tomato slices around the avocado like flower petals. If it is Spring, go outside and collect real flowers to decorate plate (do not eat flowers). Yield: 4 servings.

perfect potato salad

Ingredients

5 medium potatoes, cooked
4 hardboiled eggs, shelled
1 teaspoon salt
½ teaspoon pepper
1 teaspoon prepared mustard
½ cup sweet pickles, chopped
½ bell pepper, seeded and chopped
1 cup light or safflower mayonnaise

Directions

When potatoes are cool, peel and cut into bite-size pieces. Place in a large bowl. Remove egg yolks from hardboiled eggs and place in a small bowl. Dice the egg whites and add to potatoes. Add mayonnaise to egg yolks and blend until smooth. Add all other ingredients to bowl of potatoes. Pour mayonnaise mixture over the top and mix gently. Chill before serving. Yield: 8 servings.

sweet-sour bean salad

Ingredients

2 cups cooked green beans, in chunks, not thin slices
1–2 cups cooked kidney beans
1 onion, chopped
1 red or green pepper, chopped
¼ cup honey or sugar
¼ cup wine vinegar
¼ cup bean liquid
¼ cup oil
1 teaspoon salt

Directions

Put the prepared vegetables in a bowl. Add the remaining ingredients, stir gently to mix, cover, and refrigerate for at least 24 hours before serving.

tangy spinach salad

Ingredients
2 bunches spinach, rinsed thoroughly and torn
1 head lettuce, rinsed and torn
2 hardboiled eggs, shelled and chopped
4 tablespoons real bacon bits
6 mushrooms sliced thinly (optional)
½ cup honey
½ cup lime juice

Directions
Place first 5 ingredients in a salad bowl and toss. Combine honey and lime juice in a small saucepan and heat until warmed and blended. Pour over salad and serve immediately. Yield: 6 servings.

Activity: Start a vegetable garden with your child. You will be amazed how willingly they will start to enjoy eating their vegetables!

salad niçoise

Ingredients
1 pound white rose potatoes,
   boiled, peeled, and either diced or sliced
1 six-ounce can cut green beans, drained
2 six-ounce jars marinated artichoke hearts,
   marinade and all
1 large onion, chopped
1 six-ounce bottle Italian salad dressing
Salad greens
1 seven-ounce can white tuna, drained
1 pound cherry tomatoes
6 hardboiled eggs, halved
1 large green pepper, cut in rings

Directions
Combine potatoes, green beans, artichoke hearts, and onion with the dressing. Marinate for several hours or overnight, stirring gently several times. Line the salad bowl with greens. Drain the marinated vegetable, saving the marinade, and spoon the vegetables on top of the greens. Place the tuna in the center and arrange the tomatoes, eggs, and green peppers around the tuna. Serve the marinade to be poured over the whole salad before serving.

chicken salad in edible bowls

Ingredients

2 cups chicken, cooked and cubed
2 ribs celery, chopped
1 green apple, cored and chopped
½ cup chopped walnuts
½ cup cubed cheddar cheese
3 minced green onions
⅓ cup mayonnaise mixed with juice from ½ lemon
1 whole lettuce

Salad Bowls

1 package of egg roll skins (about 7x7)
3 inches of hot oil

Directions

Lay egg roll skin flat on the surface of oil. Submerge, pressing with a soup ladle to form bowls. When brown and crisp, drain upside down on paper towels. Mix all salad ingredients and serve on top of torn lettuce in the cooled salad bowls. Yield: 8–10 servings.

spinach and pine nuts salad

Ingredients
½ cup pine nuts
5 tablespoons extra virgin olive oil
1 clove garlic
1 shallot, minced
3 pounds fresh spinach, washed and stemmed
1 tablespoon freshly squeezed lemon juice
Pinch of ground nutmeg
Sea salt and ground black pepper

Directions
Preheat oven to 350°F (180°C). Spread the pine nuts on a baking sheet and toast for 3 to 5 minutes, until lightly browned. Heat 2 tablespoons of the oil for one minute in a fry pan. Add the garlic and shallot and sauté for 1 minute. Add the spinach and sauté, turning constantly until wilted— about 1 to 2 minutes. Add the pine nuts, the remaining 3 tablespoons of oil, and lemon juice, tossing thoroughly for 1 minute. Season with the nutmeg and salt and pepper. Transfer immediately to a serving dish and serve. Yield: 4–6 servings.

matchstick salad

Ingredients

3 slices whole grain bread
½ pound (250 g) cooked ham
1 head lettuce
4 hardboiled eggs, shelled and quartered
1 cup cherry tomatoes
4 tablespoons butter, melted
2 carrots, peeled
Favorite salad dressing
1 can shoestring potatoes

Directions

Brush both sides of bread with butter. Toast in 350°F (180°C) oven for 5 minutes on each side. Cut toast into half-inch croutons. Cut ham and carrots into matchsticks. Tear lettuce and place in salad bowl. Top lettuce with ham, eggs, tomatoes, carrots, croutons, and shoestring potatoes. Toss with salt, pepper, and salad dressing. Yield: 6 servings.

Note: A simple oil and vinegar dressing works best, but we have found that our kids prefer a creamier dressing, so we keep a supply of buttermilk or ranch dressings on hand.

snow crab salad

Ingredients
Fresh lettuce
8 ounces (225 g) snow crab
Favorite dressing
Tomatoes, sliced and cut in half
2 hardboiled eggs
4 ounces (110 g) frozen peas

Directions
Rinse and tear lettuce leaves into small pieces. Cut tomatoes into wedges. Peel and slice eggs. Toss lettuce, crab, tomatoes, and peas together. Pour dressing over salad and toss once more. Serve with French bread. Yield: 4–6 servings.

apple raisin salad

Ingredients

½ cup whole wheat flakes
½ cup chopped raisins
½ cup diced or chopped apples

Directions

Soak raisins overnight. Mix ingredients together and serve. Yield: 1 serving.

Note: Talk to your children about the food you are preparing. Comment on the taste, smell, texture and origin. Encourage children to taste the food ingredients as the meal is prepared.

ring around of jell-o

Ingredients

1 envelope unflavored gelatin
2 tablespoons honey
1½ cups apple or orange juice
1½ cups grated carrots
8 ounces (225 g) crushed pineapple
1 tablespoon lemon juice

Directions

In medium bowl, mix gelatin with honey. Heat 1/2 cup of the juice to boiling; add to the gelatin and stir until gelatin is completely dissolved. Stir in the remaining ingredients. Pour into a 1 quart round mold (or shallow square dish) and chill until firm. Yield: 6 servings.

Activity: Save the leafy end of the carrots and start a "Veggie Jungle." Put the carrot cut end down in a shallow tray with small stones and wait for new leaves to sprout. The tops of radishes and turnips will work too.

sandwiches

Mary had a little ham
a little bread, a little jam
a little mayo, a little cheese
stuck between two little leaves
looked peculiar, tasted great
that little sandwich Mary ate.

giant baked sandwich

Ingredients
8 slices bread
Butter or margarine for spreading
8 slices cheese
4 slices ham
4 eggs
½ teaspoon salt
½ teaspoon mustard
1½ cups milk

Directions
Preheat oven to 350°F (180°C). Spread bread slices with butter. Make 4 sandwiches with ham and cheese slices with buttered side on the outside. Trim edges. Place sandwiches in a greased 9-inch square pan and top with remaining slices of cheese. Beat together eggs, salt, mustard, and milk. Pour over sandwiches. Bake for 35 to 45 minutes or until custard is set and cheese starts to brown. Serve warm. Yield 4–6 servings.

Note: Other ingredients can be added to these sandwiches. Children can help decide what would taste best.

honeymoon sandwich

Ingredients
Slices of bread, any kind
Lettuce
Mayonnaise
Salad dressing
Other sliced or grated vegetables

Directions
Spread bread with salad dressing or mayonnaise. Layer on 2 or 3 lettuce leaves and any of the other vegetables. Cover with another slice of bread. Trim crusts if desired.

Note: Guidelines for children's table manners were first published in 1530. Erasmus of the Netherlands wrote about the importance of instilling manners at an early age. "If you cannot swallow a piece of food," he wrote, "turn 'round discreetly and throw it somewhere."

fruity bagel sandwich

Ingredients
2 bagels, split and toasted
3 ounces (100 g) softened cream cheese
1 peach, thinly sliced
1 banana, thinly sliced
¼ cup lemon juice
4 slices honeydew melon
¼ teaspoon cinnamon (optional)

Directions
Spread the bagels with cream cheese and sprinkle with cinnamon. Dip the peach and banana slices in lemon juice. Layer the fruit on the bagels and serve with melon slices. Yield: 4 servings.

Note: Plain, egg, whole grain, or raisin bagels are best in this recipe. Bagels, by the way, are very low in fat and are liked by most kids.

blt sandwich

Ingredients
4 slices toasted whole grain bread
4 lettuce leaves, rinsed
1 large ripe tomato
4 strips lean bacon, cooked
1 tablespoon natural mayonnaise

Directions
Spread mayonnaise on each slice of toast. Cover 2 slices with lettuce, sliced tomatoes, and 2 strips of bacon. Place toast on top, cut each sandwich diagonally, and secure each triangle with a toothpick. Yield: 4.

Note: Chores are an important part of a child's life and should not be a cause of parent-child conflict. Children need not be rewarded for doing a job. However, compliments and happiness are important. Chores are an expected part of the child's contribution to the family unit and can provide the base upon which responsibility and high self-esteem are built.

sandwich filling ideas

Ingredients
Variety of whole wheat, white, and grain breads

Fillings
Grated cheese and grated carrot
Tuna and sweet corn
Feta cheese, sliced cucumber, and fresh mint or basil leaves
Shredded chicken with cranberry jelly
Sliced beef and chutney
Ham, tomato, and relish
Cottage cheese and chopped dates or pineapple
Egg salad and mesclun salad
Sliced turkey and coleslaw
Hummus and chopped olives
Cheddar cheese and pesto
Sardines and tomato slices
Sliced fresh pear and candied walnuts

raisinut sandwich

Ingredients
½ cup peanut butter
½ cup cream cheese
1 tablespoon honey
¼ cup raisins
1 tablespoon orange juice

Directions
Blend the peanut butter and cream cheese together. Add honey, raisins, and orange juice. Mix well. Spread on whole wheat or raisin bread and serve open-faced with a glass of milk or natural apple juice. You can also keep the raisins separate and have kids make faces on their open-faced sandwiches. Yield: 8 servings.

Note: The sandwich was invented in England in the 1700s and named after the Earl of Sandwich, who wanted to keep playing cards while he ate.

egg salad sandwich

Ingredients
2 hard-boiled eggs, shelled
2 tablespoons light mayonnaise
¼ teaspoon dry mustard
¼ teaspoon salt
Pepper to taste
1 tablespoon finely chopped parsley

Directions
Chop eggs into a small bowl and mash with a fork. Add remaining ingredients and blend well. Serve on cracked wheat or other whole grain bread. Yield: 4 servings.

Note: In Jane Cooper's book, *Love at First Bite*, she suggests adding one or more of the following to egg salad: pickle relish, crumbled bacon, toasted sunflower seeds, bean sprouts, grated carrot, chopped celery, chives, raisins, chopped ham, or fresh herbs. (New York: Alfred A. Knopf, 1977).

ploughman's lunch

Ingredients
2 French bread rolls
4 thin slices of ham, beef or turkey
2 thick slices of Swiss cheese
1 ripe tomato, sliced
2 leaves of lettuce
Sweet pickled gherkins or onions

Directions
Split and spread rolls with butter or margarine. Layer meat, cheese, tomato, and lettuce on one half, put the other half roll on top. Serve on a platter with sweet pickles and coleslaw. Yield: 4 servings.

Note: During preschool and kindergarten years, the correct attitude about chores is built mostly by parent modeling and parents working with the child. All children can be expected to clean up messes they make, tidy their rooms, and make their beds.

seafood sandwich

Ingredients

1 can salmon, water processed
½ cup sour cream or light mayonnaise
1 small onion, finely chopped (optional)
½ cup cucumber, peeled and chopped
1 tablespoon lemon juice
¼ teaspoon salt
1 tablespoon sweet relish or pickles

Directions

Drain salmon. Combine all ingredients together in a bowl and mash with a fork until evenly blended. To serve, spread between slices of your favorite natural grain bread. Yield: 4–6 servings.

Note: Make your time spent in the kitchen with your children pleasurable and interesting. Don't worry about the mess and don't worry about making a perfect dish. Use the time, however short or long, to share the joys of cooking.

banana and honey sandwich

Ingredients
Slices of whole wheat or whole grain bread
Natural honey, whipped or plain
Ripened bananas

Directions
Spread slices of bread with honey. Either place banana slices on top of honey, or mash banana and spread on bread. Top with another slice of bread or eat as an open-faced sandwich. These sandwiches can be cut into small pieces for younger children.

Note: Bees may travel between 40,000 and 80,000 miles to make a pound (500 g) of honey. Some fly as far as a mile from the hive to seek the nectar from which honey is made.

grilled cheese sandwiches

Ingredients
8 slices of whole wheat or whole grain bread
2 tablespoons butter or margarine
4 slices of cheese

Directions
Preheat an electric or regular frying pan to medium heat. Butter one side of each bread slice. Take 4 slices and place them butter side down in the frying pan. Top each with a slice of cheese. Place the remaining bread on top of the cheese, buttered sides up. Evenly brown the sandwiches and flip over to other side. When golden brown on both sides remove from pan. Cut diagonally and serve with a glass of milk or juice and slices of fresh fruit. Yield: 8 servings.

sentence sandwiches

Ingredients
Alphabet cereal
Sliced wheat bread
Fruit jam

Directions
Spread the slices of bread with fruit jam. Spread a handful of the cereal on a plate and then select appropriate letters to form words and simple sentences. Apply these to the bread slices. Serve as after school or Saturday snacks.

Note: My children especially liked it when their name was spelled out on the bread and the message said "Welcome home," or "I love you," or "Feed the cat, please."

tortilla sandwiches

Ingredients
1 packet fresh whole wheat tortillas
1 small can of vegetarian refried beans
½ cup mild salsa
1 cup grated cheese

Directions
Warm tortillas according to directions on packet. Spread half the tortillas with beans then drizzle salsa over the top. Sprinkle with grated cheese. Place remaining tortillas on top of cheese and press down gently. Cut each tortilla sandwich into quarters and serve with fresh fruit slices and a lemon drink. Yield: 5–6 servings.

Note: Keep tortillas on hand and fill them with sandwich spreads, preserves, peanut butter, or thin slices of meat for a quick snack or lunch dish.

pinwheel sandwiches

Ingredients

Thin sliced bread of any kind
Sandwich spreads, such as:
   Tuna salad
   Egg salad
   Cheese spread

Directions

Prepare the sandwich spreads—the more colorful the better. Cut the crusts off the slices of bread and roll the slices flat with a rolling pin. Spread 1 tablespoon of spread on the bread. Starting with one side, roll the bread up. Slice the roll into wheels and arrange on the child's plate. Garnish with parsley and carrot curls.

Pinwheel sandwiches can be made with other filings including peanut butter and jelly, cinnamon sugar, and apple butter. These are great party sandwiches.

kid's steak sandwiches

Ingredients
2 tablespoons butter or margarine
1 large onion, sliced
1 pound (500 g) thin roast beef slices
8 ounce (250 g) jar of cheese spread
6 medium French bread rolls, split

Directions
Sauté or microwave onions in butter until tender. Add meat and heat through. Warm cheese spread in small saucepan or microwave until smooth. Fill rolls with meat and onions. Top with cheese spread. Serve with fresh fruit slices or cut up raw vegetables. Yield: 6 servings.

Note: For very small children, use dinner rolls instead of French rolls. Cut the beef into bite-size pieces before adding to onions. Children prefer thin-sliced tender meats that do not take a long time to chew.

sprinkle sandwiches

Ingredients
Sliced bread
Butter, margarine, or cream cheese
Sprinkles or cake decorations

Directions
Spread the bread with butter, margarine, or cream cheese. Lightly sprinkle with the cake decorations or colored sprinkles. Cut into triangles and serve. For parties or special occasions, the bread can be cut into shapes before decorating. These make colorful snacks at children's parties.

Note: I used to love these as a child, only back then my mother spread a thin layer of sweetened condensed milk on the bread before adding the sprinkles, which we used to call "hundreds and thousands."

soups

Tomato, potato, split pea, or rice
Black bean and barley with pinches of spice
Broths of onion, chowders of clam
Noodles with chicken, turkey or lamb
Delicious aromas so steamy and hot
come from the soups you create in a pot!

egg rice soup

Ingredients

3 cups chicken broth
1 can evaporated milk
2 egg yolks
1 cup cooked white or brown rice
½ teaspoon salt
Pepper to taste

Directions

Heat chicken broth in a saucepan. Beat egg yolks and milk together. Pour ½ cup of broth into egg mixture then pour mixture in a thin stream back into the broth in the saucepan. Heat gently until soup thickens slightly, stirring frequently. Add rice and season with salt and pepper. Serve warm with pretzel sticks or whole wheat croutons. Yield: 4 servings.

cowboy's corn chowder

Ingredients
3 tablespoons butter
1 clove garlic, minced
2 large onions, chopped
4 cups vegetable or chicken broth
½ teaspoon thyme leaves
1 bay leaf
1 pound thin-skinned potatoes
1 pound (450 g) frozen whole kernel corn, thawed
1½ cups shredded sharp cheddar cheese
½ cup whipping cream
2 cups milk
Salt and pepper
Crackers

Directions
Melt butter in a 6-quart pan over medium heat. Add garlic and onions; cook stirring, until onions are soft. Stir in broth, thyme, and bay leaf; bring to boil. Cut potatoes into half-inch cubes. Add to boiling broth; reduce heat, cover, and simmer until potatoes are tender. Stir in the corn, milk, and cream. Stir over low heat; do not let soup boil. Season to taste with salt and pepper. Put cheese in a bowl to pass at the table. Kids love to sprinkle cheese and float crackers on top. Yield: 8 servings.

alphabet tomato soup

Ingredients
3 cloves garlic, minced
1 tablespoon oil
5 tomatoes, peeled and coarsely chopped
2 quarts (2 liters) vegetable or chicken broth
¾ cup alphabet pasta
1 teaspoon dill or thyme
Salt and pepper to taste

Directions
Sauté the garlic in oil, stirring constantly until golden. Add the remaining ingredients, bring to a boil then cover and simmer 10 to 15 minutes. Yield: 8 servings.

Note: Every child should decide for himself how much, if any, he is to eat of the foods that have been prepared for him, state Genevieve Painter and Raymond Corsini in their book *The Practical Parent*. They add that he should be allowed to serve himself from serving dishes (New York: Simon and Schuster, 1984, p. 56).

split pea swirl

Ingredients
1 cup green split peas
2 quarts water
½ cup tomato sauce
1 onion, chopped
2 stalks celery, chopped
2 carrots, chopped
½ teaspoon oregano
Salt and pepper to taste
2 tablespoons sour cream

Directions
Wash and soak peas for an hour before cooking. Drain and put in a large saucepan. Add water and bring to a boil. Skim top. Simmer, covered, for another hour. Add remaining ingredients except sour cream. Simmer one more hour. Ladle into soup bowls. Place a teaspoon of sour cream in center and using a knife, swirl. Serve with bagel chips or crusty French bread. Yield: 6–8 servings.

matzo ball soup

Ingredients
6 cups chicken or beef stock
2 eggs
3 tablespoons softened butter or margarine
¾ cup matzo meal or cracker meal
½ teaspoon salt
⅛ teaspoon ginger or nutmeg
1 tablespoon parsley, finely chopped

Directions
Pour the stock into a large saucepan and heat. Beat the egg yolks and butter in a bowl until thick. Pour ½ cup of hot stock over the egg mixture and blend well. Gradually add the meal, salt, spice, and parsley, stirring constantly. Beat the egg whites until stiff, but not dry. Fold the egg whites into the matzo meal mixture and set aside. Chill if possible. About 30 minutes before serving, heat stock to boiling then reduce to simmer. Shape dough into small balls and drop them into simmering broth. Cook covered for 15 minutes. Ladle into soup bowls. Yield: 6 servings.

shrimp bisque

Ingredients

2 tablespoons unbleached flour
2 tablespoons butter
3 cups skim milk
¼ cup onion, finely chopped
¼ cup celery, finely chopped
Salt and pepper to taste
¼ teaspoon paprika
1 pound (500 g) cooked baby shrimp

Directions

Blend butter and flour in a saucepan or microwave. Gradually stir in milk and heat until thickened. Cook onion and celery until tender. Drain and add to sauce. Stir in salt, pepper and paprika. Simmer, stirring often, for 5 minutes. Fold in shrimp and heat through. Serve with crackers, unsalted pretzels, or "goldfish" crackers. Yield: 4 servings.

fresh tomato soup

Ingredients
2 tablespoons butter or margarine
1 onion, peeled and chopped
3 ripe tomatoes, peeled and chopped
3 tablespoons tomato paste
2 tablespoons unbleached flour
2 cups chicken broth
Salt and pepper to taste
1 cup milk or half and half

Directions
Melt butter in a saucepan and add onion. Sauté for 3 minutes. Stir in tomatoes and tomato paste. Cook for 3 minutes, stirring well. Gradually add flour and mix well with a wooden spoon. Slowly add the broth, salt, and pepper, stirring constantly. Simmer 15 minutes. Remove from heat and pour mixture into blender. Blend at high speed for 1 minute. Return to saucepan and add the milk. Heat through and simmer for another 2 minutes. Ladle into soup bowls and garnish with sprigs of parsley and serve with whole wheat croutons. Yield: 4 servings.

potato and popcorn soup

Ingredients

1 ounce butter
1 onion, very finely chopped
3 shallots, finely chopped
1 pint chicken stock
2 teaspoons fresh thyme
1 pound smoothly mashed potatoes
4 tablespoons white wine
Salt and pepper to taste
2 cups popped popcorn

Directions

In a large heavy saucepan over medium-high heat, melt the butter. Add the onion and shallots and cook, stirring, for about 3 or 4 minutes or until soft but not browned. Stir in the stock and thyme and bring to a boil, stirring occasionally. Gradually stir in the potatoes. Bring to a boil again. Reduce the heat to low, stir in the wine, and simmer for 5 minutes. Season with salt and pepper. Put the soup into bowls and garnish with popcorn. Yield: 4–6 servings.

chunky cream of vegetable soup

Ingredients
4 cups mixed vegetables: cauliflower, peas,
   potatoes, carrots, beans, broccoli, celery, etc.
2 tablespoons butter or margarine
2 tablespoons unbleached flour
2 cups milk
Salt, pepper, and nutmeg to taste

Directions
Rinse vegetables and chop into bite-size pieces. Steam until cooked, but still firm. Put ⅔ of the vegetables in a blender and puree. In a large saucepan, melt the butter over low heat and stir in flour to form a paste. Gradually add the milk and stir until smooth, increasing the heat until boiling. Reduce heat and add pureed vegetables. Blend in the remaining steamed vegetables and add salt and pepper to taste. Before serving, sprinkle nutmeg on top. Serve with breadsticks. Yield: 4 servings.

Note: Kids don't appreciate stringy celery. For this recipe, chop celery very finely and do not puree.

chicken dumpling soup

Ingredients
4 cups chicken stock
1 cup cooked chicken, chopped
½ cup carrots, chopped
½ cup celery, chopped
½ cup onion, chopped

Dumplings
1 cup unbleached flour
2 teaspoons baking powder
½ teaspoon salt
1 egg, beaten
⅓ cup milk

Directions
Prepare soup by adding vegetables and chicken to broth in a large saucepan. Bring to a boil then simmer for 15 minutes. Sift the flour, baking powder, and salt into a bowl. Mix together the egg and milk and add to the dry ingredients. Stir until blended. Drop tablespoons of the dough into the soup, dipping spoon into stock first. Cover tightly and steam for 10 minutes. Test with a toothpick for doneness; if it comes out clean, the dumplings are done. Yield: 4 servings.

Note: The secret to making light dumplings is to keep them steaming on top of the simmering soup. Use a glass lid to watch the dough swell.

macaroni soup

Ingredients

1 quart (1 liter) vegetable stock
2 teaspoons butter
½ cup macaroni
2 tomatoes, finely cubed
¼ cup fresh chopped parsley
Other chopped quick-cooking vegetables such as:
   sliced mushrooms, frozen peas, or
   finely chopped spinach

Directions

Bring the stock to a boil. Add the butter, any additional vegetables, and macaroni and simmer until the pasta is tender, about 10 minutes. Cut the tomatoes into small cubes then add them and the chopped parsley to the soup. Bring it back to a boil, then serve immediately. Small cubes of tofu can also be added when you add the tomatoes. Yield: 4 servings.

Note: An outrageous book for parents and kids to read is Delia Ephron's *How to Eat Like a Child* (Ballantine Books, 1978), in which she humorously describes lessons in not being a grown-up.

potato-leek soup

Ingredients
3 potatoes
3 cups cleaned, chopped leeks
1 stalk celery, chopped
1 large carrot, chopped
4 tablespoons butter
1 teaspoon salt
½ cup stock or water
3 cups milk

Directions
Scrub the potatoes clean, then cut them into 1 inch cubes. Put in saucepan with the leeks, celery, carrot, and butter. Add salt. Cook the vegetables, stirring over medium heat until the vegetables are cooked (about 5 minutes). Add the stock or water, bring to a boil, then cover, and reduce heat to a simmer. Cook until the potatoes are soft (about 20 minutes). Check to make sure there is enough water; add more if needed. When the potatoes are tender, remove the pan from heat and puree its contents in the milk (use a blender). Return the smooth mixture to the saucepan. Add any additional herbs to the top as well as salt and pepper to taste. Serve immediately. Yield: 4–6 servings.

minestrone soup

Ingredients
1 medium onion, chopped
1 stalk celery, diced
1 large carrot, sliced
3 tablespoons butter or margarine
1 large potato, peeled and chopped
2 large tomatoes, peeled and cut
2 cans beef broth
1 teaspoon dried basil
½ cup uncooked macaroni
2 small zucchinis, sliced
1 can kidney beans, drained
Salt and pepper
Parmesan cheese

Directions
In a 5-quart saucepan over medium heat, cook onion, celery, and carrot in margarine, stirring constantly until onion is soft, but not browned. Add potato, tomatoes, broth, and basil. Bring to a boil then reduce heat. Cover and simmer for 15 minutes. Add macaroni and zucchini. Cook another 10 minutes. Add kidney beans and cook another 5 minutes. Season to taste with salt and pepper. Ladle into bowls and sprinkle Parmesan cheese on top. Yield: 6 servings.

Note: This soup is delicious and is a meal in itself.

chunky vegetable beef soup

Ingredients
4 cups beef broth
½ cup uncooked rice or barley
2 carrots, diced
2 stalks celery, chopped
1 small zucchini, sliced
3 tablespoons butter
3 tablespoons flour
1 cup milk
2 tablespoons parsley, minced
1 cup chopped cooked beef (leftover steak or roast)
Salt and pepper to taste

Directions
Bring broth to a boil in a large saucepan. Add rice or barley, cover, reduce heat, and simmer for 10 minutes. Add carrots, celery, and zucchini. Cover and simmer until vegetables are crisp yet tender, about 10 minutes. In a small saucepan, melt butter. Blend in flour and cook, stirring until bubbly. Gradually pour in milk and then stir in 1 cup of the hot broth from soup. Cook until sauce boils and thickens. Stir sauce into soup, blending well. Add meat, parsley, salt and pepper to taste. Cook until just heated through. Serve with whole wheat breadsticks or crusts of French bread. Yield: 6 servings.

carrot and parsley soup

Ingredients

2 ounces (50 g) butter or margarine
1 cup carrots, peeled and grated
1 small onion, chopped finely
2 tablespoons parsley, chopped
¼ cup lentils
4 cups chicken stock
Salt and pepper to taste

Directions

Melt butter in a saucepan and cook the onion and carrot for 4 minutes over medium heat. Stir in the lentils. Cook another 2 minutes. Add the chicken stock and bring to the boil. Cover and simmer gently for 20 minutes or until the lentils are tender. Moments before serving, stir in the parsley and season with salt and pepper. Yield: 4 servings.

broccoli soup

Ingredients
1 package chopped broccoli, cooked
4 chopped green onions

White Sauce
¼ cup butter
¼ cup flour
2 cups milk
8 ounce package cream cheese
1 chicken bouillon cube
Salt and pepper to taste

Directions
To make white sauce put butter, flour, milk, cream cheese, bouillon, and salt and pepper into a saucepan. Heat over medium heat until mixture thickens. Mix broccoli, green onions, and white sauce in a blender. Blend until smooth. Reheat if necessary. Yield: 4–6 servings.

meatless chili soup

Ingredients
½ cup onion, chopped
¼ cup green pepper, diced
2 cloves garlic, minced
2 cups tomatoes, chopped
or 16 ounce can tomatoes, chopped
1 teaspoon chili powder
1 teaspoon salt (if using fresh tomatoes)
16-ounce can red kidney or pinto beans
4 small round sourdough loaves
1 cup cheese, shredded

Directions
In heavy saucepan or skillet, brown onion, green pepper, and garlic in 2 tablespoons vegetable oil until tender, stirring frequently. Add tomatoes, chili powder, and salt, and heat to boiling. Cover and simmer for 20 minutes. Stir in beans and heat through, about 10 minutes. Bake bread loaves, then cut out the middles. Save bread for dipping. Fill loaves with chili soup and cover with cheese. Yield: 4 servings.

snacks

On a cracker or a chip
In a spread or with a dip
After breakfast, after lunch
all my snacks must have a
"CRUNCH!!!"

cheese pretzels

Ingredients
1 cup flour
2 tablespoons grated Parmesan cheese
½ teaspoon salt
½ cup butter or margarine
1 cup shredded sharp cheddar cheese
2–3 tablespoons cold water

Directions
Preheat oven to 425°F (215°C). In a large bowl, stir together flour, Parmesan cheese, and salt. Using a pastry blender or 2 knives, cut in butter until mixture resembles fine crumbs. Stir in cheddar cheese. Sprinkle water over flour mixture, 1 tablespoon at a time, stirring lightly with a fork until dough holds together. Shape dough into a ball, cut in half, cutting each half into 12 parts. Place each piece of dough on a lightly floured surface; roll back and forth with palms to make a strand. Shape into designs. Bake 12 minutes.

deviled eggs

Ingredients
6 eggs, hard-boiled and shelled
1 tablespoon light mayonnaise
1 tablespoon soft margarine
1 tablespoon natural, plain yogurt
1 teaspoon Parmesan cheese
1 teaspoon Worcestershire sauce

Directions
Cut eggs in half lengthwise and remove yolks. In a small bowl, mash the egg yolks and stir in the remaining ingredients until blended. Spoon mixture into empty eggs. Place halves together to make filled whole eggs. Yield: 6 servings.

Note: To tell if an egg is raw or cooked, spin it on a flat surface. If it wobbles and barely spins, then it is raw. A hard-boiled egg will spin fast and easily.

puff pastry cheese twists

Ingredients
8 ounces (225 g) packaged puff pastry
1 egg
¾ cup grated Parmesan cheese

Directions
Preheat oven to 400°F (200°C). Roll out pastry a fourth-inch thick on a lightly floured surface to a neat square. Using a sharp knife, cut into strips 5 inches by ½ inch. Brush the strips with beaten egg and sprinkle with cheese, covering pastry evenly. Twist each pastry strip to form a spiral. Place on greased cookie sheet and bake for 7 to 10 minutes or until golden. Good for lunch box snack! Yield: 12–15 servings.

Note: Good eating habits can be easily learned when meals are planned to give a balanced diet and children are allowed to eat what they wish from what is placed before them. This is good advice from therapists Genevieve Painter and Raymond Corsine in *The Practical Parent* (New York: Simon & Schuster, 1984, p.59).

toothpick tidbits

Ingredients
Cheese cubes
Pineapple chunks
Carrot sticks
Celery sticks
Cherry tomatoes
Prunes or dates
Apple wedges

Directions
Prepare ingredients for eating. Arrange in small bowls or on a serving platter. Place toothpicks or cocktail stirrers in a holder. Have the children pierce 2 or 3 of the ingredients of their choice with a toothpick or stirrer and discover a taste treat. Yield: varies.

Note: Toothpicks are very dangerous in the hands and mouths of very young children. Keep them out of reach!

nacho popcorn

Ingredients
¼ cup butter or margarine, melted
½ teaspoon paprika
½ teaspoon cumin
¼ teaspoon red pepper
10 cups popped popcorn
½ cup Parmesan cheese

Directions
Add the spices to the melted butter and stir until blended. Toss the popcorn in a large bowl with the butter mixture and the Parmesan cheese until well-blended. Store in an airtight container if not eaten immediately. Yield: 12 servings.

Note: Corn popping is at least 5,000 years old and was originally perfected by the American Indians, who cultivated three kind of corn: sweet corn for eating, field corn for cattle feed, and so-called Indian corn for popping.

bologna lilies

Ingredients
Thin sliced white or brown bread
Slices of bologna
Mayonnaise
Thin asparagus spears, fresh or cooked
Toothpicks

Directions
Trim the crusts from the bread slices and halve each slice into two triangles. Cut the bologna slices to match the shape of the bread triangles. Spread mayonnaise on the bread and top with the meat. Roll up the bread and then place a small piece of the asparagus down the center. Secure with a toothpick.

hideout crunchies

Ingredients

⅓ cup light corn syrup
⅓ cup peanut butter
2 tablespoons sugar
1½ cups puffed wheat or corn cereal
1 cup popcorn
½ cup Spanish peanuts or raisins

Directions

Heat syrup, peanut butter, and sugar in a large microwavable bowl at high until mixture comes to a boil (about 2 minutes). Stir in remaining ingredients. Cool slightly. Wet hands with cold water and shape into small balls about the size of golf balls. Store wrapped in wax paper. Yield: 20–30 crunchy balls.

Note: To cook on the range-top, bring first 3 ingredients to a full boil stirring constantly. Pour over remaining ingredients in a large bowl. Cool and shape as directed above.

avocado half shells

Ingredients
½ cup yogurt or sour cream
1 tablespoon honey
2 apples, cored and diced
½ cup raisins
¼ cup slivered almonds
½ cup diced celery
2 avocados
1 tablespoon lemon juice

Directions
Mix together the yogurt and honey. In a large bowl, toss the mixture with the apples, raisins, almonds, and celery. Chill in the refrigerator until just before snack time. Halve and peel the avocados. Sprinkle the flesh with lemon juice. Spoon the apple mixture into the avocado halves and place on lettuce leaves if desired. Yield: 4 servings

Note: Did you know that a child will eventually eat 5,000 pounds of food in a lifetime? That is equivalent to the weight of one large elephant!

berry bagels

Ingredients

1 package dry active yeast
1 tablespoon honey
1 cup warm water
4 cups high-gluten flour
1 teaspoon salt
2 eggs

2 tablespoons vegetable oil
¼ cup sun-dried blueberries
¼ cup sun-dried cranberries
2 tablespoons water
1 egg yolk

Directions

Preheat oven to 375°F (190°C). In a bowl, place yeast, honey and warm water. Let stand for 5 minutes. Yeast must foam; if water is too hot or too cold it will not foam and the process has to be repeated. Add 1 cup of the flour, salt, and 2 eggs to the mixture. Gradually add the remaining flour, mixing with your hands. Knead the dough for 5 minutes. Coat a large bowl with half the vegetable oil. Place dough in bowl and cover with damp cloth. Let rise at room temperature for 30 minutes. Cut dough into 14 equal pieces and allow to rise another 20 minutes. Work the sun-dried berries into the dough pieces. Let little fingers poke a hole in the center and shape into a bagel. Heat a large pot of unsalted water to boiling. Lower to a simmer. Place the bagels in the simmering water for 3 to 4 minutes. Turn over and simmer another 3 minutes. Grease pan. Beat 2 tablespoons of water with the egg yolk. Brush each bagel with the egg wash and place on the baking pan. Bake for about 35 minutes or until golden brown. Yield: 14 bagels.

new zealand pikelets

Ingredients
10 ounces (275 g) unbleached flour
2 teaspoons baking powder
2 tablespoons sugar
1 egg, beaten
½ cup milk
1 tablespoon melted butter

Directions
Preheat an electric frying pan or griddle to medium-high heat. Sift together the dry ingredients in a bowl. Beat together the egg and milk and pour into the center of the flour mixture. Add melted butter. Stir until blended and add more milk if too thick. Drop tablespoonfuls onto the greased frying pan. When bubbles appear, flip over and brown other side. Cool on a wire rack and serve with butter and jam. Yield: 24 servings.

Note: My mother would have hot pikelets ready for us after school and a whole batch would disappear in seconds!

graham crackers

Ingredients
3 cups whole wheat flour
¼ teaspoon salt
½ teaspoon baking powder
¼ teaspoon cinnamon
6 tablespoons butter
¼ cup honey

Directions
Preheat oven to 375°F (190°C). Sift together flour, salt, baking powder, and cinnamon into a bowl. Melt the butter and honey together, pour this into the dry ingredients. Mix, then push the dough together with your hands. Don't knead or over mix. Place the dough on a floured surface and roll it with a floured rolling pin to ⅛ inches thick. Cut rectangles (about 2x3 inches) with a knife, and prick them with a fork. Place on a lightly greased baking tray, and bake for just 10 minutes. Cool on a rack. Yield: 3 dozen.

crispy cheese critters

Ingredients
1 packet whole wheat flour tortillas (10 or 12)
2 cups grated cheese
½ cup bacon bits
Assorted cookie cutters

Directions
Cut out shapes in the tortillas with cookie cutters. Place shapes on cookie tray or broiler pan. Arrange the grated cheese on the shapes and then sprinkle bacon bits on top. Place tray under broiler for 3 to 5 minutes or until cheese is melted and bubbly. Allow to cool slightly before serving. Yield: 24 snacks.

Note: Leftover tortilla pieces can be cut up and baked in the oven to make tortilla chips.

sweet potato chips

Ingredients
3 large yams
Oil for frying
Salt

Directions
Peel yams and slice crosswise as thinly as possible. Soak the slices in a big bowl filled with ice and water for half an hour. Drain thoroughly then dry with paper towels. Heat a half-inch oil in skillet until almost smoking. Fry chips several at a time (don't crowd) till golden, turning them once. Drain on paper towels, blotting to remove excess oil. Salt to taste and serve when cool enough. The same process can be followed to make potato chips.

asparagus rolls

Ingredients
Slices of fresh brown bread
Butter or margarine, softened
Asparagus spears, steamed and cooled

Directions
Thinly spread butter on bread slices. Trim off the crusts. Place an asparagus spear on one side of each bread slice. Roll up. Place seam side down on a cutting board. Cut each roll into 3 small ones and arrange on a serving platter. Garnish with sprigs of parsley. Yield: Varies.

disappearing artichoke dip

Ingredients
2 cans (15 ounces) artichoke hearts, cut up
1 cup real Parmesan cheese, grated
1 cup mayonnaise

Directions
Preheat oven to 350°F (180°C). Mix ingredients together and bake in oven for 30 minutes uncovered. Serve with crackers or a brown and serve bread loaf baked then cut in small squares for dipping.

Note: In her book *Your Child's Self Esteem*, Dorothy Corkille Briggs states that helping children build self-esteem is the key to successful parent-hood (New York: Doubleday, 1975, p. 6).

toasted pumpkin seeds

Ingredients
1 cup fresh pumpkin seeds
2 tablespoons butter or margarine, melted
Seasoned salt to taste

Directions
Preheat oven to 325°F (160°C). Rinse pumpkin seeds and pat dry. Spread seeds on a cookie tray. Drizzle with the butter and lightly sprinkle with salt. Bake for 1 hour or until seeds are brown and crisp. Turn seeds often. Yield: 1 cup.

Note: Be certain to use seeds from pumpkins that have not been treated with herbicides or fungicides.

crispy tartlets

Ingredients
2 sheets phyllo pastry
1 egg white
½ cup ricotta cheese
Fresh basil leaves
3 small tomatoes, quartered
Salt and pepper to taste

Directions
Preheat oven to 400°F (200°C). Brush the sheets of pastry lightly with egg white and cut into 16 4-inch squares. Layer the squares in pairs and place each pair in 8 muffin cups. Spoon the soft cheese into pastry shells. Season with pepper and add one or two basil leaves. Arrange tomato wedges on top of leaves and lightly sprinkle salt on top. Bake for 10–12 minutes, until pastry is golden brown. Serve warm. Yield: 8 tartlets.

cookies

Busy little fingers
kneading out the dough
baking oatmeal cookies
as fast as they can go.

Flour on the ceiling
thumbprints on the walls
smudges on their faces
batter in the halls.

Splashes of vanilla
a dozen eggshells too
cups of powdered sugar
have dropped upon their shoe.

When the fun is over
and they go off to rest
guess who is left behind
to clean up their mess?

detective cookies

Ingredients
½ cup brown sugar
½ cup butter
1 teaspoon vanilla
2 eggs
2½ cups unbleached flour
2 teaspoons baking powder
½ teaspoon salt

Directions
Cream sugar, butter, vanilla, and eggs. Mix in flour, baking powder, and salt. Chill dough for 3 hours. Preheat oven to 375°F (190°C). Roll dough out on floured surface. Cut with shaped cookie cutters. Place thumb on top of cookie and press thumb to make a thumbprint. Bake 7 to 10 minutes. Yield: 24 cookies.

Note: Try making a story up about each cookie. Then pretend to be detectives investigating the case! For example, your cookie is working at a toy shop, and is going on a trip. Find out where!

oatmeal raspberry bars

Ingredients
½ cup softened butter or margarine
⅓ cup light brown sugar
1 cup unbleached flour
¼ teaspoon baking powder
⅛ teaspoon salt
1 cup rolled oats
¾ cups natural raspberry jam

Directions
Preheat oven to 350°F (180°C). Grease a square pan. Mix all the ingredients together except the jam. Press 2 cups of the mixture into the bottom of the pan. Spread the jam close to the edge. Sprinkle the remaining oatmeal mixture over the top and press lightly. Bake 25 minutes and allow to cool before cutting into bars. Yield: 16–24 bars.

Note: Try the new fruit-only jam in this recipe for a real taste of summer raspberries. This fruit-sweetened jam is not quite as sweet as sugar-sweetened jams, but much more healthful!

chocolate pinwheels

Ingredients
1 cup butter or margarine, softened
1 cup sugar
3 eggs
1 teaspoon almond extract
3 cups unbleached flour
1 teaspoon baking powder
¼ teaspoon salt
2 tablespoons carob powder or unsweetened cocoa powder

Directions
Preheat oven to 350°F (180°C). Beat butter and sugar in a large bowl. Add beaten eggs and almond extract. Blend in sifted flour, baking powder, and salt and stir until a dough is formed. Divide into 2 balls and set on waxed paper. Add the carob powder to one ball and knead until blended evenly. On a lightly floured surface, roll each ball into a rectangle. Place the rectangles on top of each other and trim sides. Roll up. Cut half-inch slices crosswise and place slices on greased cookie tray. Bake 10 to 12 minutes. Yield: 24 cookies.

peanut kiss cookies

Ingredients
½ cup Crisco shortening
½ cup natural peanut butter
½ cup white sugar
½ cup brown sugar
1¾ cups unbleached flour
1 teaspoon baking soda
½ teaspoon salt
2 tablespoons milk
1 teaspoon vanilla
Chocolate or carob kisses

Directions
Preheat oven to 350°F (180°C). In bowl, mix shortening, peanut butter, and sugars until smooth. Add flour, baking soda, and salt. Mix. Add milk and vanilla. Make dough into 1½-inch balls and roll them in sugar. Bake 8 minutes on ungreased cookie sheet. Put chocolate or carob kiss on top and bake for another 3 minutes. Yield: 24 cookies.

pineapple apple bars

Ingredients
15-ounce can unsweetened crushed pineapple
1⅓ cups apple, chopped
¾ cup brown sugar
1½ cups unbleached flour
1 teaspoon baking soda
1 egg, beaten
¼ teaspoon ginger

Directions
Preheat oven to 350°F (180°C). Stir together dry ingredients in a bowl. Combine remaining ingredients in another bowl, stirring well. Pour liquid mixture into flour mixture and mix until just blended. Spoon into a 9x13 baking pan. Bake 40 minutes or until a toothpick comes out clean. Cool before cutting into squares. Yield: 24 bars.

some more's

Ingredients
Small bag of marshmallows
5 milk chocolate candy bars
20–30 graham crackers

Directions
Toast a marshmallow over a fire. If you don't have an outdoor flame, toast over a gas or electric stove top on metal sticks, or quickly in the microwave (5 seconds). Put the toasted marshmallow on the graham cracker, top with a piece of chocolate and cover with another graham cracker. Always a camper's favorite!

chocolate brownies

Ingredients
½ cup mashed banana
⅓ cup vegetable oil
2 eggs
½ teaspoon vanilla extract
¼ cup milk
1 cup unbleached flour
¼ cup whole wheat flour
¼ cup carob or cocoa powder
¼ teaspoon baking soda
⅔ cup rolled oats

Directions
Preheat oven to 350°F (180°C). In a bowl, beat together the banana, oil eggs, milk, and vanilla until creamy. Beat in flour, carob powder, and baking soda. Stir in the oats and mix thoroughly. Grease a cookie sheet and drop batter by the teaspoonful onto the cookie sheet. Bake 8 to 10 minutes. Don't over bake; they are done when just firm to the touch. Cool and serve. Yield: 3 dozen.

gingerbread giants

Ingredients

1 cup molasses
6 tablespoons butter
2 tablespoons water
½ cup brown sugar
1 teaspoon each: cinnamon, ginger
½ teaspoon each: nutmeg, cloves
½ teaspoon baking soda
½ teaspoon salt
3 cups whole wheat pastry flour
½ cup powdered milk

Directions

Preheat oven to 350°F (180°C). Pour molasses into a small pan. Heat until it bubbles around the edge. Put butter in mixing bowl and pour molasses on top. Stir. Add water, brown sugar, cinnamon, nutmeg, cloves, ginger, salt, and baking soda. Stir until mixed, then add flour and milk. If dough is too sticky, add more flour. Dip hands in water and begin to shape your giants. Place giants on greased cookie sheet. Use raisins, chocolate chips, icing, etc., to decorate. Bake 12 minutes or more depending on size of giants. Yield: 6–8 giants.

Note: Play a dancing game while you design your cookies—you can even shape your giants with dancing arms and legs like you!

chewy fruit cookies

Ingredients
²⁄₃ cup butter
2 teaspoons vanilla
1 egg
1³⁄₄ teaspoons baking powder
Pinch of salt
½ cup unbleached flour
½ cup wheat flour
1 cup shredded unsweetened coconut
½ cup dried pineapple, chopped
1 cup chopped dates
²⁄₃ cup wheat germ

Directions
Cream together the butter, vanilla, and egg. Gradually beat in the dry ingredients and mix thoroughly. Mix in the dried fruits. Roll the dough into 2 logs about 1½ inches in diameter. Roll the logs in the wheat germ to coat them. Wrap in waxed paper and chill until firm enough to slice. Preheat oven to 350°F (180°C). Slice cookies a half-inch thick and place on a greased cookie sheet. Bake 10 minutes until golden brown. Yield: 4 dozen.

puppet show cookies

Ingredients
1⅓ cups butter or margarine
⅔ cup sugar
1 teaspoon vanilla
3 cups unbleached flour
Vegetable food coloring
10 wooden sticks

Directions
Beat butter until soft. Add sugar and beat until fluffy. Add vanilla. Gradually add flour and beat until mixture resembles coarse crumbs. Divide the dough into several parts, depending on the colors you choose. Add a few drops of color to dough and knead with hands. Form dough into puppet characters, about a half-inch thick and 6 inches tall. Carefully insert a stick about 2 inches up. Bake at 350°F (180°C) for 20 minutes. Cool completely before playing with them. Yield: depending on size, about 10 puppet cookies.

Note: This is a fun party activity—have kids put on a puppet show after their puppets have cooked!

lemon bars

Ingredients
½ cup vegetable oil
4 eggs
6 ounces frozen pineapple juice concentrate
⅓ cup fresh lemon juice
2 cups unbleached flour
¼ cup wheat germ
1 teaspoon baking powder

Directions
Preheat oven to 375°F (190°C). Beat together the oil, eggs, pineapple concentrate, and lemon juice. Add flour, wheat germ, and baking powder, and beat. Drop by tablespoon onto a greased cookie sheet. Bake for 8 minutes until tops are firm but not brown. Cool and eat. Yield: 2 dozen.

chocolate chippers

Ingredients
1 cup butter or margarine
¾ cup brown sugar
½ cup white sugar
1 teaspoon vanilla
2 eggs, or 1 egg and ¼ cup sweetened condensed milk
2¼ cups unbleached flour
½ teaspoon salt
1 teaspoon baking soda
1 cup milk chocolate or carob chips

Directions
Preheat oven to 350°F (180°C). Cream butter, sugars, egg, and vanilla until fluffy. Mix in flour, salt, and baking soda. Add chocolate chips. Drop by tablespoons onto a greased cookie sheet. Bake for 12 to 15 minutes. Yield: 24 cookies.

rice mallow bars

Ingredients
¼ cup butter or margarine
10 ounces (300 g) marshmallows
4 cups puffed rice cereal
½ cup carob or chocolate chips

Directions
Melt butter and marshmallows together in a large saucepan over medium heat. Stir until blended. Add rice and chips and stir quickly until mixed. Put mixture into a greased 8x8 pan. Wet hands with water and push down to fill pan. Chill before serving and cut into squares with a wet knife. Yield: 24 bars.

Note: The first candy bar was a Hershey chocolate bar in 1894.

miss ginger snap

Ingredients
½ cup butter
¼ cup margarine
2 cups brown sugar
2 eggs
½ cup molasses
1 teaspoon each: cinnamon, ginger, and nutmeg
3¾ cups unbleached flour
2 teaspoons baking soda

Directions
Cream butter and margarine. Beat in sugar. Add eggs and molasses. Stir in remaining ingredients. Chill for several hours. Preheat oven to 350°F (180°C). Roll into 1-inch balls. Place on lightly greased cookie sheets. Bake for 8 minutes. Cool and eat! Yield: 3 dozen.

pie crust rolls

Ingredients

2 cups unbleached white flour
½ teaspoon salt
⅔ cup shortening
2 tablespoons butter or margarine
4 tablespoons melted butter
¼ cup sugar
2 teaspoons cinnamon

Directions

Preheat oven to 350°F (180°C). Work the shortening and butter together with fingertips. Add flour and salt. Cut with a pastry cutter or 2 knives until a soft dough forms. Roll dough out on a floured surface. Spread melted butter on top of dough and then sprinkle with a mixture of sugar and cinnamon. Roll up like a jelly roll. Cut crosswise into half-inch slices. Bake on a lightly greased cookie tray for 8 minutes or until light brown. Yield: 24 rolls.

Note: These rolls can be made with leftover pastry when you are making a pie. Children can make the rolls with you.

chocolate peanut butter surprise cookies

Ingredients
4 cups coconut
½ cup oatmeal
2⅓ cups walnuts, chopped
5 cups dates, chopped
1½ cups whole wheat pastry flour
¼ teaspoon salt
1⅓ cups cold water
1½ cups peanut butter
½ cup honey
2 teaspoons vanilla extract

Directions
Preheat oven to 350°F (180°C). Mix all ingredients in a large bowl. Line cookie trays with heavy waxed paper. Use an ice cream scoop to place mixture on paper. Bake for 25 minutes or until golden brown. Yield: 4 dozen cookies.

orange cookies

Ingredients

4 oz. (1 stick) butter or margarine, softened
1 cup sugar
2 egg yolks
1 tablespoon fresh orange juice
Grated rind of 1 orange
1½ cups all purpose flour
½ teaspoon salt
1 teaspoon baking powder

Directions

In a large bowl, cream the butter and sugar with an electric mixer until light and fluffy. Add the egg yolks, orange juice, and rind. Blend well. In another bowl, sift together the flour, salt, and baking powder. Add this mixture to the butter mixture and stir until it forms a smooth dough. Wrap the dough in waxed paper and chill for 2 hours. Preheat the oven to 375°F (190°C). Grease two baking sheets. Roll spoonfuls of the dough into balls and place 1–2 inches apart on the baking sheets. Press each ball with a fork to flatten. Bake for 8–10 minutes, until golden brown. Transfer to a rack to cool. Yield: 20–30 cookies.

Note: The orange can be replaced with other citrus fruits, such as tangerines or tangelos. All are rich in vitamin C.

designer foods

A pancake is the head
Ten raisins are the toes
Two berries make the eyes
A carrot for the nose
It's not a great Picasso
Sassoon or Calvin Klein
It's just a funny recipe
I call my OWN design.

designer pancakes

Ingredients
1½ cups low-fat milk
4 tablespoons vegetable oil
2 eggs
2 teaspoons baking powder
1½ cups flour
Oil or butter for frying

Directions
Put ingredients in a bowl and mix. Heat skillet over medium heat; add 2 tablespoons of oil. When a drop of water dances on the surface of the skillet you are ready to begin your art! Using a large spoon, dribble the pancake mix into the skillet, making a design. Make sure to make your designs small enough to fit inside a pancake. Cook design for 30 seconds. Pour ¼ cup of the remaining batter on top of the design and wait until pancake has bubbles on it before turning it over (1 to 2 minutes). Turn pancake and brown other side. Cover with syrup or jam and eat! Yield: 4 servings.

oatmeal add-ons

Ingredients
2 cups water
1 cup rolled oats (if using instant, follow instructions on box)
¼ teaspoon salt
¼ cup dried fruit pieces (optional)

Directions
Bring salt and water to a boil. Add oatmeal and cook until it begins to thicken (1 to 2 minutes). Reduce heat and simmer for 10 minutes, stirring occasionally. Pour oatmeal into bowls and place on table. Put all the add-on ingredients into small bowls and suggest that your children make a picture on the top of the oatmeal. After picture is complete, stir up the oatmeal and eat. Only one rule to the game; they have to eat their creation! Yield: 4 servings.

Add-Ons
Raisins
Coconut
Pineapple tidbits
Sliced bananas
Any other favorite small food

taco salad

Ingredients
Bag of Fritos
Can of refried beans
Cheese of your choice
Lettuce
2–3 tomatoes
Sour cream
1 pound ground beef, cooked and drained

Directions
Put all ingredients out on the counter. Have children layer them in whatever order they would like in a rectangular pan (sized according to how many people you are serving, and the amount of ingredients). Serve. Yield: 6–10.

collage melt

Ingredients
Thinly sliced meats
Thinly sliced cheese
Whole grain bread
Tomato
Boiled eggs
Other favorite toppings

Directions
Butter the slices of bread and place face down on a cookie sheet. Use scissors to cut the meat and cheese into small shapes. Slice tomato and eggs into small pieces. Have your child decorate each bread slice making colorful collages. Put the cookie tray under the broiler for a few minutes until the cheese melts and the shapes all run together. Cool and eat.

Activity: After you finish lunch, do some stretching exercises together, up, down, and side to side. Try stretching each other!

terrific tomato soup

Ingredients
1 can tomato soup
¼ cup natural plain yogurt

Garnishes
Popcorn
Pretzels
Corn chips
Crackers
Grated cheese

Directions
In a saucepan, cook the soup according to directions on the can. Pour into bowls. Have yogurt and garnishes ready in separate bowls. Spoon yogurt onto soup and then encourage your child to create designs or patterns with the garnishes. Yield: 4 servings.

Note: This is a good experiment to observe which foods float and which ones sink!

heavenly star pizza

Ingredients
Favorite cheese
English muffins, split and toasted
Pizza or spaghetti sauce
Optional:
    Turkey or tofu hot dog slices
    Pineapple
    Chopped bell pepper
    Onion
    Tomato

Directions
Preheat oven to 350ºF (180ºC). Cut cheese slices into star shapes with a cookie cutter. For each serving, spread muffin half with sauce. Let child top pizza with favorite additions. Bake for 10 minutes or until cheese is melted and browned. Yield: Varies.

cracker crunchies

Ingredients
Assorted crackers
Apple, sliced
Cheese spread
Berries
Cucumber, sliced
Avocado, peeled and sliced
Eggs, hardboiled and shelled
Cream cheese

Directions
Start with the crackers and let your child's imagination run free with the toppings. Children enjoy helping to prepare their own party dishes, so let them create and arrange the cracker tray.

mashed potato sculpture

Ingredients
8 potatoes
4 tablespoons butter
4 tablespoons milk
2 teaspoons salt
2 egg whites

Directions
Boil potatoes until tender. Cool. Peel and mash with an electric mixer.
Add milk, salt, and butter. Let cool in refrigerator. Butter a large baking
dish and empty potatoes into it. Using toothpicks, teaspoons, forks,
popsicle sticks and clean fingers, form potatoes into shapes. Try animals,
faces, etc. Beat egg whites slightly and spread over the sculptures with a
pastry or clean paint brush. Bake until brown and shiny. Yield: 6 servings.

Game: Take turns making sounds. Can you guess what the sound is?
Oink!

designer omelet

Ingredients
2 eggs per person
1 tablespoon milk for every 2 eggs
Salt and pepper to taste
Finely chopped tomatoes
Finely chopped cooked ham or chicken
Grated cheese
Chopped leftover vegetables

Directions
Preheat skillet. Beat the eggs with milk in a small glass measuring cup. Add salt and pepper to taste. Place the remaining ingredients in separate small bowls. Pour the egg mixture in the skillet and swirl until most of the skillet bottom is covered. Scramble the eggs so they are mostly cooked, then spread them to cover the skillet bottom. Turn the heat low. Ask your child to select and then arrange the fillings on top of the egg mixture. Cook for 3 to 5 minutes and then fold the omelet in half so that filling is enclosed. Cook for another 2 minutes with the lid on. There is no need to flip the omelet over. Slide onto a warm plate and serve immediately.

food sculpture

Ingredients
3 ounces (75 g) cream cheese
3 tablespoons sour cream or plain yogurt
Onion soup mix
Snack foods: chips, popcorn, pretzels, crackers, etc.

Directions
Warm cream cheese until soft. Blend in 3 tablespoons sour cream and mix in ½ packet of soup mix. Arrange the snacks in piles, then proceed to build a sculpture, selecting from the assortment of snacks and cementing them together with the cheese spread. The cheese doesn't add much strength so it is best to keep the sculpture low. When finished, your child can have fun eating his or her creation!

clubhouse sandwiches

Ingredients
8 slices white and whole wheat bread
Assorted sandwich fillings:
  Peanut butter
  Lettuce
  Tomato slices
  Cheese slices
  Chicken or turkey slices
  Alfalfa sprouts
  Cream cheese
  Tuna salad
  Egg salad
  Watercress

Directions
Trim the crusts off the bread slices. Place the sandwich fillings on separate plates. Alternate white and whole wheat bread slices and let child choose the fillings to go between 4 slices. Cut into squares or triangles and secure each section with a toothpick. Yield: 8 servings.

Note: Remember to use toothpicks with care.

peach perfection

Ingredients
1 can peaches
1 package Jell-O, any flavor
1 package vanilla pudding mix
1 container non-dairy whipping cream
Toppings, such as coconut, cherries, or sprinkles

Directions
Drain the peaches and reserve liquid. Add cold water to peach juice to make one cup. In a heat-proof pitcher, dissolve Jell-O in 1/2 cup of boiling water. Add juice and water mixture. Pour Jell-O into four glasses and chill until jelled. Just before serving, prepare pudding mix, chop peaches, thaw non-dairy whipping cream, and put toppings in bowls. Remove glasses from refrigerator and let child layer ingredients according to taste. Yield: 4 servings.

Note: Fresh fruit in season can be used instead of canned peaches and toppings can include cereals, finely chopped nuts, and crushed cookies.

designer fish tacos

Ingredients
8 soft corn tortillas
1½ lbs. of cooked (steamed or baked) cod fillets
1 teaspoon ground ginger
3 teaspoons fresh lemon or lime juice
6–8 lettuce leaves, torn into small pieces
Avocado, peeled and diced
Apple (Granny Smith), peeled, cored and diced
½ onion, peeled and diced
Sprig of parsley, chopped finely

Directions
Wrap the tortillas in aluminum foil and warm in a 400°F (200°C) oven for 5 minutes or until warm and softened. In one bowl, combine the cod, ginger and 2 teaspoons of the lemon juice and toss. Season to taste. In another bowl, combine the apple, avocado, onion, parsley, and 1 teaspoon of the lemon juice. Toss well. To serve, spoon the fish mixture onto the warm tortilla, then top with some lettuce and the apple and avocado mixture. Yield: 4 servings.

layered vegetable salad

Ingredients

1 cup broccoli flowerets
1 cup grated carrot
1 cup shredded lettuce
1 cup cauliflower flowerets
1 cup cooked green peas
1 cup creamy herb or ranch salad dressing

Directions

Place prepared vegetables in separate bowls. Give each child a clear plastic or glass salad bowl. Alternately layer the vegetables to suit taste with an eye towards design. Spoon salad dressing over top of salad or alternate a layer of dressing with vegetables. Serve with a sandwich and a glass of milk. Yield: 6 servings.

monkey bread

Ingredients

1 cup milk, scalded
1 cup cooked mashed potatoes
½ cup vegetable oil
½ cup honey
½ teaspoon salt
1 packet dry yeast
2 eggs, beaten
5–6 cups unbleached flour
2 tablespoons butter, melted

Directions

Combine milk, potatoes, oil, honey, and salt in a large bowl. Dissolve yeast in ½ cup lukewarm water. Add the eggs and yeast to potato mixture. Stir in 2 cups flour and mix well until blended. Gradually add the remaining flour until a stiff dough forms. Turn out and knead thoroughly. Return to a greased bowl and turn over. Cover and let rise in a warm place until double in size, about 2 hours.

Punch down and divide into quarters. Grease a deep baking dish or tube pan. Pinch off small pieces of dough and dip in melted butter. Arrange in pan in layers and let rise until double. Meanwhile, preheat oven to 400°F (200°C). Bake bread for 25 minutes or until hollow-sounding when tapped. Serve while still warm and let the children pull the bread apart to eat. Yield: 12 servings.

tortilla towers

Ingredients

1 pound (225 g) ground beef
½ teaspoon seasoned salt
1 can Mexican style stewed tomatoes
1 can tomato sauce
2 tablespoons Spanish tomato sauce
½ teaspoon oregano
16 ounces (500 g) cottage cheese
2 eggs
1 can refried beans
12 corn tortillas
2 cups Monterey Jack cheese, grated

Directions

Preheat oven to 350°F (180°C). Brown and drain ground beef. Add salt, tomatoes, sauce, and oregano. Blend and simmer 20 minutes. Cool. Combine cottage cheese and eggs. Empty beans into a bowl. Spread 1 cup of meat sauce in rectangular dish, size depending on how high the towers will be. Build towers by alternating meat mixture, cottage cheese mixture, beans, and tortillas. Top with grated cheese. Bake for 30 minutes. Let stand 5 minutes before cutting into wedges. Serve with a salad and Spanish rice. Yield: 8 servings.

kids' kebabs

Ingredients
Baby onions
Cherry tomatoes
Green pepper
Pineapple chunks
Mushrooms
Grapes
Boneless chicken, beef, or pork, cubed

Marinade
Mix together in a bowl:
3 tablespoons brown sugar
2 tablespoons soy or tamari sauce
2 cloves garlic, crushed
1 onion, sliced very fine

Directions
Prepare barbeque grill. Make the marinade (see below) and chill. Cut the ingredients into bite-size pieces. Place meat in marinade to coat. Place all ingredients in separate bowls and arrange on barbeque table. Give each person a skewer and let each one design a kebab. Grill kebabs four inches above glowing coals, turning once or twice until cooked. Slide kebab off onto warm plates and serve with couscous and a crisp green salad. Yield: varies.

pasta

Oregano and garlic
Sauce by the oodles
Tomato and basil
Fresh pasta noodles

Bend crinkle spiral twirl
loop wrinkle twist curl

An original recipe
From Jennie and Kate
WIGGLE WORM SPAGHETTI
Piled on their plate.

macaroni and cheese

Ingredients
½ pound (450 g) macaroni
2 tablespoons margarine
2 tablespoons flour
2 cups milk
1 teaspoon mustard
1 cup grated cheddar cheese

Directions
Preheat oven to 400°F (200°C). Put four quarts cold water in a large pot and boil. Sprinkle macaroni into boiling water and cook ten minutes. To make the sauce, melt margarine over medium heat, stir in flour with a whisk. Add milk and cook, stirring constantly with the whisk, until it is slightly thickened with no lumps. Remove from heat, stir in 1 teaspoon salt, pepper, mustard, and cheese. Drain the macaroni and place in a greased casserole dish. Pour sauce over and bake for 20 minutes. Yield: 6 servings.

homemade noodles

Ingredients
2 cups unbleached flour
5 eggs
1–2 tablespoons olive oil

Directions
Sift the flour in a pile onto a work surface. Make a well in the center of the flour. Break the eggs into the center, add the oil, mix with a fork, and work the dough with hands until smooth and elastic (a good job for small, clean hands). Roll out with a rolling pin, until very thin. Leave the pasta to dry for 5 to 10 minutes then sprinkle with flour and roll up the sheet of pasta gently. With a knife, cut into thin strips. Sprinkle with flour. Cook in boiling water until pasta floats to the top and is tender. Serve with butter, Parmesan cheese, sauce, or anything else your child likes on noodles. Yield: 4–6 servings.

Activity: Save all the empty cartons you cooked with today and let your child build something out of them as you make dinner.

spaghetti and meatballs

Ingredients

1 pound (500 g) ground beef
⅓ cup bread crumbs
1 egg
½ cup ketchup
½ cup oatmeal
Salt and pepper to taste
1 pound (500 g) spaghetti
Parmesan cheese
Favorite spaghetti sauce

Directions

In a large bowl, combine the beef, bread crumbs, egg, ketchup, oatmeal, salt, and pepper. Mix with hands until well-mixed. Wet hands and shape meat mixture into small meatballs, about 1½ inches in diameter. Cook in skillet over medium heat until meatballs are browned on all sides and cooked through. Boil water for spaghetti noodles. When meatballs are done, place on paper towel to remove excess grease. Cook spaghetti according to package directions. When done, drain and return to pot. Pour sauce over noodles and heat through. Add meatballs. Sprinkle with Parmesan cheese and serve. Yield: 6–8 servings.

zucchini and yogurt pasta

Ingredients

1 pound (500 g) zucchini
½ pound (250 g) pasta, ribbons, or your favorite shape
3 cloves garlic, crushed
1 tablespoon butter
1½ cups yogurt
½ cup sour cream
1 teaspoon salt
½ teaspoon honey or sugar
1 teaspoon paprika
3 tablespoons freshly chopped parsley
1 tablespoon lemon juice
Parmesan cheese

Directions

Cut the zucchini into slices, not more than a half-inch thick. Put the pasta on to cook, using instructions on the packet. Sauté the zucchini with the crushed and chopped garlic, until it has softened and is beginning to turn golden. Remove from the heat and add the yogurt, sour cream, and seasonings. Stir gently until everything is well combined. Stir into the cooked pasta and serve hot. Sprinkle individual servings with Parmesan cheese if desired. Yield: 4 servings.

flowering spinach lasagna

Ingredients
1 jar of spaghetti sauce (26 ounces)
10 ounces frozen chopped spinach, thawed
2 cups ricotta cheese
1 cup mozzarella cheese, shredded
1 egg, beaten
¼ teaspoon pepper
½ teaspoon salt
¼ teaspoon nutmeg
12 lasagna noodles
Parsley

Directions
Cook lasagna according to package directions. Drain and cool. Squeeze water out of spinach. In a bowl, mix together spinach, cheeses, egg, pepper, salt, and nutmeg. Pour spaghetti sauce into a greased shallow casserole. To assemble flowers, spread 2–3 tablespoons of cheese mixture on noodle and roll up like a jelly roll. Place flowers, curly side up, in the casserole in the sauce. Cover and bake at 350°F (180°C) for 30 minutes or until heated through. Garnish with sprigs of parsley. Yield: 12 servings.

chicken fruit pasta salad

Ingredients
8 ounces (225 g) pineapple chunks
4 halved chicken breasts, cooked and cut into bite-size pieces
1 stalk celery, chopped
1 cup seedless grapes
8 ounces (225 g) rotelle (pasta shaped like twists)

Pineapple Mayonnaise
1 tablespoon pineapple juice, drained from can
½ cup mayonnaise
1 teaspoon fresh lemon juice

Directions
Drain pineapple chunks and reserve juice for dressing. Prepare pineapple mayonnaise. Place chicken, celery, grapes, and pineapple in a large bowl; refrigerate until ready to use. Cook pasta according to package directions. Drain and rinse with cold water. Add pasta to chicken mixture, cover with pineapple mayonnaise. Salt and pepper to taste. Yield: 4 servings.

lovely lemon noodles

Ingredients
1 pound (500 g) spaghetti
½ cup butter
1 pint sour cream
Juice of one large lemon
1 teaspoon grated lemon peel
¼ cup minced parsley
Parmesan cheese
Fresh ground pepper to taste

Directions
Preheat oven to 400°F (200°C). Cook the noodles in boiling water, drain and put into a baking dish. Melt butter in a small pan and remove from heat. Stir in the sour cream, lemon juice, and peel. Pour over pasta, mix, and bake 20 to 25 minutes. Remove from the oven and sprinkle parsley, Parmesan, and pepper on top. Toss lightly and serve. Yield: 6 servings.

Note: When you have dinner all ready and almost everything on the table, play this little game before dinner. Ask your child what is missing on the table. It could be someone's fork or napkin or glass. Reverse roles and let your child remove something and you guess what's missing.

wild rice with apples

Ingredients

½ pound (250 g) wild rice, cooked according to package
½ cup butter, melted
2 tablespoons minced onion
1 large green apple, peeled, cored and chopped
1 cup fresh bread crumbs
½ cup chopped walnuts
¼ cup dried apricots, or other dried fruit finely chopped
¼ cup fresh orange juice

Directions

Preheat oven to 325°F (170°C). Melt butter and use 1 tablespoon of it to sauté onion. Add to cooked rice. Add remaining ingredients and mix well. Put in a 2 quart casserole dish. Cover and bake 35 minutes. Serve warm. Yield: 8 servings.

Activity: As you cook and eat, communicate only through songs.

donna's noodle rice

Ingredients

½ cup butter or margarine
5 fideo noodles, crunched
2 cans chicken broth
1 cup uncooked rice
¼ cup water

Directions

Melt butter in large frying pan. Lightly brown fideo noodles. Add broth, water, and rice. Bring to a boil then reduce to simmer. Cover and cook over low heat for 30 minutes or until rice is soft. Yield: 6 servings.

Activity: Have your child make a centerpiece for the dinner table. Fill a shallow bowl with sand and arrange twigs, flowers, and dried grasses in it.

gnocchi

Ingredients
5 tablespoons butter
½ cup unbleached flour
2¼ cups chicken broth
2 eggs
½ cup grated Parmesan cheese
¼ teaspoon nutmeg
¾ cup tomato sauce
3 tablespoons cream
1 teaspoon basil

Directions
Melt butter in a small pan and stir in the flour. Add the broth and stir vigorously. Cook, stirring constantly, until the mixture draws away from the sides of the pan. Remove from heat. Stir in the eggs (one at a time), cheese, and nutmeg. Heat water to boiling in a large pan and drop the dough into the water by the teaspoon. Cook for 10 minutes. Strain. Add tomato sauce, cream, and basil. Cook until warmed and serve. Yield: 4 servings.

lazy lasagna

Ingredients
1 box lasagna noodles
2 cups spaghetti sauce
2 cups mozzarella cheese
1 cup ricotta or cottage cheese
1 pound (500 g) ground beef, cooked and drained
¾ cup water

Directions
This is called lazy lasagna because the step of cooking the noodles before assembly has been dropped. In a greased rectangular cake pan, place one layer of noodles on the bottom. Cover with meat, cheeses and sauce. Layer another layer of noodles and repeat until all ingredients are gone. Pour water over the top. Cover with foil and bake at 350°F (180°C) for 45 minutes. Remove foil and bake another 10 to 15 minutes. Let set 10 minutes before eating. Yield: 10 servings.

white rice

Ingredients
2 cups water
½ teaspoon salt
1 tablespoon butter
1 cup long grain white rice
Optional additions: beans, nuts, vegetables, eggs, seasoning, etc.

Directions
Place water in saucepan; add salt and butter. Bring to a boil. Stir in the rice. Reduce heat to low, cover tightly, and simmer without removing cover for 20 to 25 minutes. If you would like to, add optional juices to water when boiling, or add additions when rice is finished. Yield: 4 servings.

Note: On cold days, rice tastes great with warm milk, brown sugar, and a dab of butter.

bacon and egg spaghetti

Ingredients
¼ cup real bacon bits
1 pound (450 g) spaghetti noodles
½ cup butter or margarine
1 peeled garlic clove
⅓ cup fresh parsley, chopped
½ cup Parmesan cheese, grated
2 eggs, beaten
2 hardboiled eggs, shelled and chopped

Directions
In a large saucepan, bring 4 quarts of water to a boil. Add spaghetti and cook for 10 minutes. While noodles are cooking, prepare sauce. Put butter and garlic in a small saucepan and melt over a low heat. Add the beaten eggs, stirring for a minute, and remove from heat. Drain spaghetti and put into a large bowl. Remove garlic from butter mixture and pour over spaghetti. Toss to blend. Sprinkle parsley, chopped egg, bacon bits, and cheese over top. Mix together and serve warm. Yield: 8 servings.

apple risotto

Ingredients

4 apples (red, green, or yellow),
peeled, cored and cut into cubes
Juice from 1/2 lemon
5 tablespoons butter
⅓ cup olive oil
1⅔ cups risotto rice
¼ cup dry white wine
4 cups vegetable or chicken broth
½ cup grated Parmesan cheese
Dash of nutmeg, salt, and pepper

Directions

Bring a pan of water and lemon juice to a boil. Immerse the apples,
bring back to a boil, and cook for 3 minutes. Drain and place in a small
pan with one tablespoon of the butter. Fry until golden brown. Remove and
keep warm. Place pan over medium heat. Put 2 tablespoons butter in a
pan with oil. Sprinkle in the rice and let it turn golden. Add the wine and
broth, bring to a boil then cover and simmer. Stir from time to time to
mix well. Add the apples after 15 minutes and continue cooking over low
heat for 10 more minutes. Just before the rice is cooked add the cheese,
salt, pepper, nutmeg, and remaining butter. Serve warm. Yield: 6 servings.

avocado pasta

Ingredients
1¼ pounds pasta, whatever shape you like
1 avocado
Juice of 1/2 lemon
Pinch of ground dried chili
Salt
6 tablespoons extra-virgin olive oil
2 ripe tomatoes, peeled and diced
1 tablespoon chopped fresh parsley

Directions
In a large pot, bring salted water to a boil. Add the pasta and cook until al dente. Meanwhile, cut the avocado in half. Remove the pit, then peel the halves and cut them lengthwise into thin slices. Place the slices in a bowl and sprinkle them with lemon juice, chili, and salt to taste. Add the olive oil and stir gently. Drain the pasta and transfer it to a platter. Pour the avocado mixture over the pasta, and then toss together gently. Sprinkle the tomatoes and parsley over the top. Serve at once. Yield: 6 servings.

rice mold

Ingredients
1 tablespoon chopped parsley
1 teaspoon chopped basil
1 clove garlic
1 onion, sliced
½ cup white wine
1⅔ cups risotto rice
1 quart (1 liter) chicken broth
¼ cup grated Parmesan cheese
2 tomatoes, sliced and peeled
7 thick slices mozzarella cheese

Directions
Preheat oven to 400°F (200°C). Finely chop the herbs and garlic together. Place the onion in a large pan with the wine and cook for 4 minutes. Sprinkle in the rice, add the broth, and simmer until the rice is al dente (about 15 minutes). Add the herbs, garlic, and cheese. Pour half the rice into a nonstick cake pan or ring mold and season with salt and pepper. Cover with slices of peeled tomato and mozzarella cheese. Cover with remaining risotto rice. Bake for 20 minutes. Turn out onto a warm serving dish. Yield: 8 servings.

diana's spaghetti pie

Ingredients
6 ounces of spaghetti
2 tablespoons butter
⅓ cup grated Parmesan cheese
2 beaten eggs
1 cup cottage or ricotta cheese
½ cup shredded mozzarella cheese

Meat Filling
1 pound (500 g) ground beef
½ cup chopped onion
8 ounce can undrained tomatoes, cut up
6 ounce can tomato paste
1 teaspoon sugar
1 teaspoon dried crushed oregano
½ teaspoon garlic salt

Directions
Cook spaghetti and combine with butter, Parmesan cheese, and eggs. Press into a buttered 10-inch pie plate. Prepare meat filling by cooking the beef and onion in a skillet over medium heat until brown. Add the sauces and spices, heat through. Spread the cottage cheese over spaghetti "crust." Fill crust with meat filling. Bake uncovered in a 350°F (180°C) oven for 20 to 25 minutes. Sprinkle with mozzarella cheese. Bake 5 more minutes. Let stand 5 minutes before serving. Yield: 6 servings.

vegetables

Brussels sprouts and corn
Asparagus and beans
Radishes and cucumbers
Most types of greens

Turnips and cabbage
Spinach and tomatoes
Onions and mushrooms
Most kinds of potatoes

Squash, peppers and
especially GREEN PEAS . . .
are just a few veggies
that cause me to sneeze!

apple potato folds

Ingredients
¾ cup unbleached flour
3 cups mashed potatoes
2 sliced, peeled apples
½ teaspoon salt
4 tablespoons butter
Cinnamon and sugar

Directions
Mix the flour and mashed potatoes together, kneading to make a pliable dough. Divide dough in half. Roll each half of the dough into a circle. Put the apple slices on one half of each dough circle. Sprinkle apples with cinnamon and sugar; dab butter on top. Fold other half of dough over apples and pinch around edges to seal. Cook over medium heat in a frying pan until apples are cooked and dough is golden on both sides. If apples take longer to cook, turn heat to low and cover. Cut into pie-shaped pieces. Yield: 10 servings.

vegetable cheesecake

Ingredients

3 cups packed coarsely grated zucchini

3 tablespoons butter

1 cup minced onion

3 cloves garlic, crushed

½ teaspoon salt

1 cup grated carrot

3 tablespoons flour

½ teaspoon each basil and oregano

1 tablespoon fresh lemon juice

3 cups ricotta cheese

1 cup grated mozzarella cheese

½ cup grated Parmesan cheese

4 eggs

4 tablespoons bread crumbs

Sliced tomatoes (for decoration)

Directions

Preheat oven to 375°F (190°C). Butter a 10" spring form pan and sprinkle in the bread crumbs, coating the bottom and sides. Set the grated zucchini in a strainer, lightly salt, and let stand 15 minutes. Squeeze out excess moisture. In a heavy skillet, sauté the onions in butter with salt. Add garlic, carrots, zucchini, flour, and herbs. Keep stirring, and cook over medium heat 8 minutes. Remove from heat; stir in parsley and lemon. Beat together cheeses and eggs. Add the sautéed vegetables and mix well. Season to taste with salt and pepper. Pour into prepared pan and bake uncovered for ½ hour. Remove from oven and arrange tomatoes decoratively on top. Return to oven, reduce heat to 350°F (180°C), and bake another 30 minutes. Turn off the oven, open the door, and leave the cake in the oven for 15 minutes. Cool 10 minutes before eating. Yield: 8 servings.

vegetables in creamy white sauce

Ingredients
1 package frozen peas
1 tablespoon butter or margarine
2 tablespoons flour
2 cups milk
Salt and pepper to taste

Directions
Cook the frozen peas according to directions on package or microwave until heated through. Drain. Make the white sauce by melting butter and stirring in the flour until mixture is smooth. Blend in ½ cup of the milk and heat, stirring constantly. Gradually add the rest of the milk and stir until mixture becomes thick and creamy. Heat until sauce just starts to boil. Add the cooked peas. Season with salt and pepper. Yield: 6 servings.

Note: Peas are a good source of protein as well as vitamins A and C.

whipped cheese potatoes

Ingredients
10 large potatoes, peeled and halved
6 ounces cream cheese
1 cup sour cream
2 teaspoons onion salt
1 teaspoon salt
½ teaspoon pepper
3 tablespoons butter

Directions
Cook potatoes in a big pot of boiling salted water until tender. Mash them until smooth. Add the remaining ingredients and beat until light and fluffy. Yield: 10 servings.

Note: My son likes to spread cold whipped potatoes on a slice of white bread or toast as a snack. He says it tastes delicious!

vegetable dip

Ingredients
Assorted raw vegetables
2 cups plain yogurt
¼ cup chutney, chopped
1 teaspoon dried mint flakes, crumbled

Directions
Rinse the vegetables and break or cut into bite-size pieces. Arrange on a large platter. Mix together the yogurt, chutney, and mint. Stir until well blended. Pour into a small bowl and place in the center of the vegetables. Have ready as an after school snack. Yield: 12 servings.

corn and carrot pudding

Ingredients

3 tablespoons butter or margarine
2 onions, finely chopped
3 tablespoons unbleached flour
½ teaspoon curry powder
½ teaspoon salt
1½ cups milk
1 cup carrots, cooked and drained
1 cup corn, cooked and drained
1 cup bread crumbs

Directions

Preheat oven to 275°F (160°C). Melt 1 tablespoon of the butter and cook onion until soft. Add flour, curry powder, salt, and lastly, milk, stirring constantly. When sauce is smooth and thick, fold in carrots and corn. Pour into an ovenproof dish. Melt remaining butter and brown bread crumbs. Spread bread crumbs over top of vegetable mixture. Bake uncovered for 30 minutes. Serve warm with fish or chicken. Yield: 4 servings.

scalloped potatoes

Ingredients
4 medium potatoes
4 tablespoons butter
4 tablespoons flour
2 cups milk
1 cup grated cheese
Salt and pepper
¼ teaspoon paprika

Directions
Preheat oven to 350°F (180°C). Peel and cook the potatoes then set aside to cool. Make 2 cups of cream sauce by melting the butter and blending in the flour. Heat gently and while stirring constantly, slowly add the milk. Keep stirring until the sauce begins to thicken. Add the grated cheese and salt and pepper to taste. Add the cut up potatoes and mix well together. Pour into a buttered casserole and sprinkle with paprika. Bake for about 10 minutes or until well heated through. Yield: 4 servings.

Note: This cream sauce can be made quickly and easily in the microwave oven in a glass bowl. Other vegetables can be used instead of potatoes, for example cauliflower, peas, or broccoli.

vegetable patties

Ingredients

1 egg, beaten
1 carrot, grated
1 onion, finely chopped
1 potato, peeled and grated
1 cup unbleached flour
1 teaspoon baking powder
¼ cup milk
Salt and pepper to taste
Vegetable cooking oil

Directions

Preheat a skillet or electric fry pan. Put all the vegetables in a bowl and stir in the egg and milk. Mix the dry ingredients together and add gradually to the vegetable mixture. Batter should be moist and fairly thick. Pour 2 tablespoons oil into fry pan. Drop tablespoons of batter into the oil. Cook until golden brown and turn over. Test the patties with a toothpick to make sure the insides are cooked through. Remove from pan onto paper towels. Serve warm with ketchup and a green vegetable. Yield: 18 patties.

golden roast potatoes

Ingredients
4 medium potatoes
2 tablespoons butter or margarine
Salt and pepper to taste

Directions
Preheat oven to 350°F (180°C). Scrub the potatoes. Peel only if marred or where green. Cut into wedges or quarters. Melt butter and brush potatoes. Sprinkle a little salt and pepper over skins. Place potatoes in a greased small roasting pan. Bake for 20 to 30 minutes or until golden brown. Potatoes can also be roasted in an electric frying pan. Try surrounding a roasting chicken or turkey with the potatoes during the last 30 minutes of cooking. Yield: 6 servings.

carrot mushroom loaf

Ingredients

1 medium-sized onion
2 cloves garlic
2 tablespoons butter
½ pound (200 g) mushrooms, sliced
1 teaspoon basil
¼ teaspoon thyme
½ teaspoon salt
Black pepper

3 cups grated carrot
½ cup dry bread crumbs
½ cup grated cheese
½ cup milk
2 eggs
2 tablespoons bread crumbs
2 tablespoons grated cheese
Paprika

Directions

Preheat oven to 350°F (180°C). Finely chop the onion and garlic, then cook in the oil or butter until the onion is soft. Add the sliced mushrooms and continue to cook until these have softened. Transfer the cooked onion and mushroom mixture to a medium-sized bowl and then add the next nine ingredients. Mix together well, then pour into a well-greased loaf tin. Sprinkle with the remaining measures of bread crumbs and cheese and dust lightly with paprika. Cover pan with foil, and bake for 30 minutes, then uncover and cook for another 30 minutes or until the center is firm when pressed.

vegetable pie

Ingredients
2 cups sliced zucchini
1 cup chopped tomato
½ cup chopped onion
½ cup grated carrot
⅓ cup grated Parmesan cheese
½ cup grated cheddar cheese
2 cups milk
1 cup biscuit baking mix
4 eggs
½ teaspoon salt
¼ teaspoon pepper
½ teaspoon sweet basil
½ teaspoon parsley flakes

Directions
Preheat oven to 400°F (200°C). Grease a 10-inch pie plate. Sprinkle vegetables and cheese in pie plate. Beat remaining ingredients until smooth. Pour into pie plate. Bake for 30 minutes until golden brown. Let stand 5 minutes before serving. Yield: 8 servings.

Note: Any assortment of vegetables could be used, just make sure they are cut in small enough pieces to be cooked through.

zucchini cakes with red pepper

Ingredients
2 eggs
1 large garlic clove
½ teaspoon salt
3 cups shredded zucchini, unpeeled
¼ cup grated Parmesan cheese
½ cup self-raising flour
Oil

Red Pepper Puree
1 onion, finely chopped
1 clove garlic, chopped
1 large red bell pepper
1 tablespoon butter
1 cup water

Directions
In a medium-sized bowl, beat the eggs. Crush the garlic clove into the salt, and add the paste to the eggs. Mix. Add the firmly packed shredded zucchini and the Parmesan cheese, then stir in enough flour to m batter of fritter consistency. Drop batter into hot oil, a fourth-inch a tablespoon at a time to make small cakes. Turn when golden h Lower heat if necessary and cook until centers are firm. Serve w pepper sauce. To make sauce, finely chop onion, garlic, and Sauté in the butter or oil until transparent. Add water, cover, a for 10 minutes, until tender. Puree. Pour over zucchini. Yield: 6 s

old-fashioned green beans

Ingredients

4–6 slices bacon
1 large onion, chopped
1½–2 pounds green beans, snapped
½ cup water
Salt and pepper to taste
6–8 new potatoes (optional)
1 cube chicken bouillon (optional)
¼ teaspoon sugar (optional)

Directions

In a heavy pot, fry the bacon until crisp over medium heat, remove the bacon, and drain. Add the onion to the bacon grease and sauté until limp. Add the green beans, water, salt, pepper, and any of the optional ingredients. Simmer the mixture, covered, for 45 minutes or until tender. Transfer the green bean mixture to a serving dish and crumble the bacon over the top. Yield: 6–8 servings.

cauliflower cheese cloud

Ingredients
1 medium cauliflower
1 teaspoon lemon juice
¼ cup butter
2 tablespoons flour
1 cup milk
3 eggs, separated
1 cup grated cheddar cheese
Salt and pepper to taste
¼ cup bread crumbs

Directions
Preheat oven to 400°F (200°C). Cook cauliflower in salted water with lemon juice until tender; set aside. Melt butter in a saucepan then add flour and cook until brown. Gradually stir in milk, egg yolks, grated cheese, salt, and pepper. Cook over low heat until mixture is smooth and thick. Break cauliflower into pieces and place in a greased 9x13-inch baking pan. Beat egg whites until stiff. Fold into cheese mixture. Pour over cauliflower. Sprinkle with bread crumbs. Bake for 30 minutes until puffy and brown.

stir-fried vegetables

Ingredients
4 tablespoons vegetable oil
2 garlic cloves, peeled and chopped
1 pound diced vegetables, such as
    cauliflower florets, bean sprouts,
    carrots, broccoli florets, onions, or mushrooms
¼ teaspoon salt
2 tablespoons water

Directions
Heat the oil in a flameproof frying pan or casserole. Add the garlic and stir until it turns golden brown. Using a slotted spoon, remove all the garlic. Add the vegetables and salt. Fry quickly, stirring, until the vegetables are coated with oil. Add the water and continue to stir-fry until the vegetables are tender but still crisp. Place the vegetables on a heated serving dish and keep warm until ready to serve. Yield: 6 servings.

hash brown heaven

Ingredients
1 pound (500 g) frozen shredded potatoes
1 cup milk
¼ cup butter or margarine
¼ cup chopped parsley
1 tablespoon dried onion flakes
½ teaspoon salt
½ cup grated cheese

Directions
Thaw potatoes. In a saucepan over medium heat, bring milk to a boil and add potatoes. Heat until liquid is absorbed. Remove from heat and add butter, parsley, onion, and salt. Transfer to a greased casserole dish. Sprinkle cheese over top. Bake uncovered for 1 hour or until golden brown on top. Yield: 6–8 servings.

asparagus crepes

Ingredients
1 pound (500 g) asparagus, steamed
  and cut into small pieces
3 ounces cream cheese

Crepe Mixture
2 eggs
¾ cup milk
½ cup flour
½ teaspoon salt

Directions
Combine eggs, milk, flour, and salt in a blender until smooth. Pour a measured 2 tablespoons into a small, smooth-surfaced, well-sprayed or buttered preheated skillet. Immediately tilt pan so batter covers bottom in a thin film. When batter no longer looks wet in the center, ease edges of crepe from pan. Lift and turn carefully. Dry second side, without browning. Remove from pan. Stack crepes until required. Spread with softened cream cheese, put asparagus slices inside, roll up, and eat. Yield: 4 servings.

meats

Nothing smells better
on a cold autumn day
than a casserole baking
in a pot made of clay.

Delicious main dishes
prepared with great care
Rich, spicy aromas
encircle the air.

Warm fires burning
Gathered 'round the rug
Families together
so cozy and snug!

mini meat pies

Ingredients

1 cup butter or margarine
1 cup cream cheese or kefir cheese
2 cups unbleached flour
½ teaspoon salt
½ pound lean ground beef
1 small onion, chopped
¼ teaspoon marjoram
1 teaspoon dry or fresh parsley, chopped
1 tablespoon dry bread crumbs

Directions

Preheat oven to 425°F (215°C). Prepare pastry by creaming together butter and cheese. Stir in flour and ¼ teaspoon salt and blend until a dough forms. Shape into a ball and chill. In a frying pan or skillet, brown meat with onion. Drain excess fat. Add remaining ingredients and ¼ teaspoon salt. Mix well. Remove from heat. Roll out pastry to ⅛-inch thickness. Cut into twelve 4-inch squares. Place 1 tablespoon meat mixture on each square and fold in half diagonally. Press edges with a fork to seal. Place pies on a lightly greased cookie tray and bake 15 minutes or until golden brown. Yield: 12 pies.

pork chops and sweet potatoes

Ingredients
6 large sweet potatoes
4 tablespoons cooking oil
6 two inch thick pork chops
Salt and pepper
6 large tart apples
1 cup golden raisins
1 teaspoon cinnamon

Directions
Preheat oven to 400°F (200°C). Peel the potatoes, cut them into large chunks and boil them until about half done. Set aside. Heat the oil, browning the pork chops quickly on both sides. Put the chops and sweet potatoes into a large baking pan. Salt and pepper. Peel, halve, and core the apples. Place them in the pan with the chops and sprinkle on the raisins. Sprinkle cinnamon on each apple. Cover the pan tightly with foil and bake 50 minutes until apples and chops are tender. Yield: 6 servings.

family pot roast

Ingredients
3–4 pound beef rump or chuck roast
1 teaspoon salt
½ teaspoon seasoned salt
¼ teaspoon seasoned pepper
¼ teaspoon paprika
1 tablespoon instant minced onion
1 cup beef bouillon

Directions
Rub all sides of meat with salts, pepper and paprika. In a slow-cooking pot (Crock-Pot), combine seasoned meat with onion and bouillon. Cover and cook on low 8 to 10 hours or until meat is tender. Remove from pot and slice. Yield: 6–8 servings.

Note: If gravy is preferred, thicken juices with 1 tablespoon flour dissolved in a small amount of water after removing meat from pot. Also, vegetables such as potatoes, carrots, onions, or turnips may be added and cooked the same time as the meat.

beef stroganoff

Ingredients
2 pounds fillet steak
2 small onions
⅔ cup sliced mushrooms
2 tablespoons butter
½ cup sour cream

Directions
Cut steak into strips about 2 inches long by a half-inch thick. Chop onion roughly. Melt butter in saucepan over medium heat. Add onion and steak and cook until steak is almost tender (about 8 minutes). Add mushrooms and cook for a further three minutes. Add sour cream and cook mixture until hot (about 5 minutes). Yield: 4 servings.

chili

Ingredients
1 pound (500 g) lean ground beef
1 packet mild chili mix
2 cans stewed, chopped tomatoes
1 can pinto or kidney beans, drained
1 onion, chopped
1 packet (4 ounces) unsalted crackers
1 cup grated cheese

Directions
Brown the ground beef in a frying pan or electric skillet. Drain off excess fat. Sprinkle chili mix over meat and stir to blend with a cup of water. Add the tomatoes. Cover and simmer for 20 minutes. Stir in the beans and heat through. Serve the chili in bowls or ramekins with the chopped onions, crackers and cheese on the side. Yield: 6 servings.

Note: Children are generally cautious when it comes to hot, spicy foods. You may want to taste-test the chili before serving. To be on the safe side, try using only 1/2 the packet of chili mix.

shepherd's pie

Ingredients

1 pound (500 g) ground beef
1 onion
1 carrot
2 cups beef broth
Salt and pepper to taste
2 cups cooked potatoes
1 tablespoon butter
¼ cup milk
4 slices cheddar cheese

Directions

Preheat oven to 350°F (180°C). Brown ground beef and drain off the fat. Add chopped onion, diced carrot, broth, salt and pepper. Simmer for 20 minutes or until meat is tender. Thicken with 2 tablespoons cornstarch dissolved in ¼ cup water. Stir until smooth and bubbling. Pour into a deep baking dish. Mash potatoes with butter and milk. Spread slices of cheese over meat mixture then pile potatoes on top, spreading to touch sides of dish. Bake for 15 minutes or until peaks of potatoes are golden brown. Cool slightly before serving. Yield: 6 servings.

chinese beef and pea pods

Ingredients
1 pound (500 g) lean flank steak
1 can condensed beef consommé (bouillon)
¼ cup soy sauce
¼ teaspoon ground ginger
1 bunch green onions, sliced
2 tablespoons cornstarch
2 tablespoons water
1 package frozen or 1 cup fresh pea pods

Directions
Thinly slice flank steak diagonally across the grain. Combine strips in crockpot with consommé, soy sauce, ginger, and onions. Cover and cook on low for 5 to 7 hours. Turn control to high. Stir in cornstarch mixed with water. Cook on high for 12 minutes or until thickened. Add the pea pods for the last 5 minutes. Serve over hot rice. Yield: 4–6 servings.

teriyaki beef kebabs

Ingredients
6 topside steaks
1 cup beef stock
¼ cup teriyaki sauce
2 tablespoons hoisin sauce
2 tablespoons lime juice
1 tablespoon honey
1 green onions, finely chopped
2 cloves garlic, crushed
1 teaspoon finely grated ginger

Directions
Trim meat of excess fat. Slice meat across the grain evenly into long, thin strips. Thread meat on skewers "weaving" them in place. Combine stock, sauces, lime juice, honey, onion, garlic, and ginger in a small bowl. Whisk for one minute or until well combined. Place skewered meat in a shallow dish, pour marinade over. Store in refrigerator, covered with plastic wrap, for 2 hours or overnight, turning occasionally. Drain, reserving marinade. Place meat on a cold, lightly-oiled grill tray. Cook under high heat for 2 minutes each side, turning once. For a rare result, cook a further 1 minute each side. For medium and well-done results, lower the grill tray or reduce heat, and cook a further 2 to 3 minutes. Brush occasionally with the reserved marinade during cooking. Yield: 6 servings.

hominy beef casserole

Ingredients
1 pound (500 g) lean ground beef
1 cup grated cheese
2 cans golden hominy
1 can tomato sauce (15 oz.)
1 medium onion, chopped
½ teaspoon salt
Seasonings to taste: pepper, paprika, garlic, oregano

Directions
Preheat oven to 350°F (180°C). Brown the meat in a fry pan or skillet. Drain excess fat. Add onion and seasonings. Stir in tomato sauce. In an ovenproof casserole dish, place layers of hominy, meat sauce and cheese. Bake for 20 minutes or until cheese is melted throughout. Yield: 6 servings.

sneaky meat loaf

Ingredients
1 pound (500 g) lean ground beef
1 cup uncooked oatmeal
1¾ cup spaghetti sauce
½ chopped onion
⅓ cup Parmesan cheese
1 egg
1 tablespoon Worcestershire sauce
½ cup shredded mozzarella cheese
½ cup of any of the following (or be creative):
  sliced mushrooms, shredded zucchini, grated cheese,
  mashed potatoes, grated carrots, cooked vegetables,
  frozen peas, sliced tomatoes, cold macaroni cheese,
  or broken potato chips

Directions
Preheat oven to 350°F (180°C). Grease a deep 8-inch round baking pan.
Combine ground beef, oatmeal, ¾ cup spaghetti sauce, onion, Parmesan
cheese, egg, and Worcestershire sauce. Mix well. Halve mixture and
shape into two circular patties, about 7 inches in diameter. Place stuffing
choice on top of one patty. Cover with the other patty and seal by
pinching sides together. Put into a pan. Bake 40 to 45 minutes. Cover
with remaining spaghetti sauce and top with mozzarella cheese. Return
to oven to melt cheese. Serve with baked potatoes and a vegetable.
Yield: 6 servings.

very easy beef stew

Ingredients
1–1½ pounds beef stew meat, cubed
3 tablespoons unbleached flour
2 tablespoons vegetable oil
3 cups water
1 packet beef stew or gravy mix
4 potatoes, scrubbed and diced
4 carrots, scrubbed and diced
2 onions, peeled and quartered
10 ounce (25 g) packet frozen peas
1 teaspoon salt

Directions
Coat the meat with flour and then brown in heated oil in a Dutch oven. Add the water and seasoning mix. Stir well and bring to a boil. Reduce heat and simmer, covered, for 1½ hours. Add all the vegetables except peas and cook another 45 minutes or until vegetables are tender. Add the peas and salt during last 5 minutes. Stir often while stew is cooking. Yield: 6–8 servings.

Note: This stew can also be prepared in a Crock-Pot.

dried fruit pork chops

Ingredients
¾ cup apple juice
½ teaspoon salt
½ teaspoon ground cloves
4 thick pork chops
1 tablespoon vegetable oil
½ cup dried cranberries or apricots
¼ cup half and half

Directions
Prepare marinade by combining apple juice, salt, and cloves in a shallow dish. Add pork chops, turning to coat. If possible, chill covered for several hours. Preheat oven to 350°F (180°C). Remove chops and brown in oil in a frying pan. Place chops in baking dish with marinade and dried fruit. Bake for 45 minutes. Remove chops and add 1/4 cup half and half to marinade, boil until a little thickened (sauce will be thin). Transfer to serving platters and top each chop with the fruit sauce. Yield: 4 servings.

barbecued baby ribs

Ingredients
1 cup barbeque sauce
½ cup soy or tamari sauce
1 cup ketchup
1 onion, peeled and minced
1 tablespoon honey
2 pounds (1 kg) baby back ribs

Directions
Prepare barbeque sauce by combining all ingredients, except ribs. Marinate ribs in the sauce overnight. To cook, preheat oven to 300°F (150°C). Place ribs and sauce in an uncovered casserole dish and bake for 1 hour or until meat separates from bones. Serve warm with a green salad and baked potatoes. Yield: 6–8 servings.

Note: The term "barbeque" comes from the French "de barbe a queue" which means "from beard to tail." In the old days, whole animals, including goats, were roasted on a spit over an open fire.

tangy apple meatballs

Ingredients

1 pound (500 g) ground beef
1 tablespoon finely diced onion
⅓ cup flour
½ cup soft bread crumbs
Salt and pepper
1 egg
1 apple, peeled and grated
1 tablespoon apple juice
1 package (50 g) potato chips, crushed
2 tablespoons oil

Sauce

2 tablespoons soy sauce
Pinch of mustard powder
¼ cup apple juice mixed with
    1 teaspoon cornstarch
½ cup vinegar
2 tablespoons sugar

Directions

Combine the meat, onion, flour, bread crumbs, seasonings, and egg. Mix the grated apple and apple juice together, then add to meat; combine well. With wet hands, form the mixture into small balls and roll the balls in crushed potato chips. Chill for 4 to 5 hours. Heat oil in a pan and shallow fry the balls for approximately 5 minutes. Makes 10 balls. To make the sauce, mix the mustard with the soy sauce, add the remaining ingredients and heat until the sugar has dissolved. Serve sauce over meatballs.

meat in a loaf

Ingredients
1 loaf French bread, unsliced
1 cup milk, scalded
1 pound (500 g) ground pork or beef
1 egg, beaten
1 small onion, chopped
1 teaspoon salt
¼ teaspoon pepper
3 tablespoons ketchup
2 tablespoons chopped green pepper
2 tablespoons chopped celery

Directions
Cut a slice from end of bread. Scoop out as much bread as possible. Measure 2 cups of bread and soak in the scalded milk. Brown meat over medium heat and drain excess fat. Add the vegetables and sauté briefly. Combine meat and vegetable mixture with seasonings, ketchup, and bread and stir until thoroughly mixed. Add beaten egg. Fill hollowed loaf with mixture, packing it in firmly. Bake on a cookie tray at 350°F (180°C) for 1½ hours. Slice with a bread knife and serve with a salad or green vegetable. Yield: 6 servings.

ham steak with pineapple

Ingredients
4 ham steaks
4 tablespoons soy sauce
4 pineapple rings (fresh if possible)

Directions
Remove any excess fat from ham steaks. Marinate ham steaks in soy sauce for at least an hour. Keep steaks covered while marinating. Grill ham steaks on medium heat for 2 to 3 minutes each side. Grill pineapple for one minute each side. Yield: 4 servings.

poultry

Chicken, Chicken, I've been thinkin'
Now's the time to scurry
Run before you're in the pot
With dumplings, rice, and curry.

honey-lover's chicken

Ingredients
4 whole boneless chicken breasts
½ cup melted butter or margarine
2 tablespoons flour
2 tablespoons prepared mustard
½ cup corn flake crumbs
½ cup yellow cornmeal
1 teaspoon salt
¼ teaspoon paprika

Directions
Preheat the oven to 350°F (180°C). Remove the skin from the chicken breast. Cut each boneless breast in half lengthwise. Blend flour and mustard into melted butter until smooth. Dip chicken pieces in butter mixture and coat well with crumbs and seasonings. Place on a shallow foil-lined pan and drip remaining butter mixture on top. Bake 35 minutes or until tender. Dip into honey and eat. Can also be refrigerated and taken for lunch. Yield: 4 servings.

chicken stroganoff

Ingredients

5 boneless chicken breast halves, skinned and cut into 1-inch pieces
Salt and pepper
3 tablespoons butter
1 medium onion, sliced
½ pound mushrooms, sliced (optional)
1 tablespoon unbleached flour
1 cup chicken broth, heated
½ cup sour cream
1 tablespoon Dijon mustard
Chopped fresh parsley
Cooked white or brown rice

Directions

Season chicken with salt and pepper. Melt 2 tablespoons butter in heavy large skillet over medium-high heat. Add chicken and cook until opaque, stirring occasionally, about 5 minutes. Transfer to serving dish. Add onion and mushrooms to skillet and cook until light brown, 6 to 8 minutes. Add to chicken dish. Melt remaining butter in small saucepan over medium-low heat. Add flour and stir 3 minutes. Whisk in broth and stir until sauce is thickened and smooth, about 5 minutes. Stir in sour cream and mustard. Heat sauce until warmed through but do not boil. Pour over chicken, top with parsley and serve with rice. Yield: 4–6 servings.

tortilla chicken dip

Ingredients
3 cups chopped cooked chicken
1½ cups grated sharp cheese
¼ cup chopped parsley
½ cup mayonnaise
1 tablespoon chopped onion
½ teaspoon cumin
1 tomato, sliced
1½ cups tortilla chips

Directions
Preheat oven to 350°F (180°C). Combine chicken, 1 cup cheese, parsley, mayonnaise, onion, and cumin. Mix lightly. Spoon the mixture into a 1½ quart casserole dish. Bake for 25 minutes. Remove from oven and top with tomatoes and remaining cheese. Arrange chips around edge of the casserole. Continue baking another 10 minutes. Yield: 4–6 servings.

cornish game hens

Ingredients
2 game hens
Favorite stuffing mix
½ cup dried cranberries
1 cup chicken broth
1 onion
3 tablespoons butter
Salt and pepper

Directions
Preheat oven to 350°F (180°C). Wash and dry the hens. Make favorite stuffing mix according to package. Mix in the dried cranberries. Stuff the hens with the stuffing mixture. Melt butter in pan you plan to cook hens in, add chopped onion and brown. Place hens in pan and pour broth over top. Salt and pepper stuffed hens. Cook breast side up for 45 to 50 minutes. To make a gravy, take hens out of the pan, cook broth over medium heat until it boils. Turn down the heat and add 2 tablespoons flour mixed into ¼ cup water. Stir until thickened. Serve in dish beside hens. Yield: 4 servings.

chicken and dumpling casserole

Ingredients
2 cups cooked chicken
3 tablespoons butter or margarine
½ cup onions, thinly sliced
½ cup celery, chopped
½ cup carrots, chopped
3 tablespoons flour
½ cup frozen peas
3 cups chicken broth

Dumplings
1 cup unbleached flour
2 teaspoons baking powder
Pinch salt
1 egg, beaten in ⅓ cup milk

Directions
Preheat oven to 400°F (200°C). Cut chicken into cubes. Melt the butter in a frying pan and lightly sauté the onions, celery, and carrots. Sprinkle the flour over the vegetables and blend into the juices. Gradually add the broth and stir as mixture thickens. Add the peas and season with salt and pepper. Pour the mixture into a greased casserole dish. Prepare the dumplings by sifting the dry ingredients into a bowl and quickly stirring in the egg mixture. Add additional flour to make a stiff dough. Divide the dough and shape into 8 balls. Drop the dough balls onto the casserole and bake uncovered 15 minutes or until biscuits are cooked through. Yield: 8 servings.

creamy chicken enchiladas

Ingredients

16 ounces plain yogurt or sour cream
1 can (250 g) cream of mushroom soup
1 small can diced green chilies
¼ teaspoon cayenne pepper
16 corn or flour tortillas
2 cups cooked chicken, shredded
16 slivers cheddar cheese
1 medium onion, peeled and chopped
1 cup grated cheese

Directions

Preheat oven to 350°F (180°C). Blend together yogurt, soup, chilies, and cayenne. Spread half of the mixture on the bottom of an 13x9 Pyrex dish. Along the center of each tortilla, place a tablespoon of chicken, a sliver of cheese and a teaspoon of onion. Roll up and place seam side down in the Pyrex dish. Continue until all tortillas are filled. Pour remaining soup mixture over the tortillas. Top with grated cheese. Bake for 20 minutes or until heated through. Serve with fluffy Spanish rice. Yield: 8 servings.

Note: Other canned soups may be used instead of cream of mushroom. Try cream of celery or chicken or potato.

chicken normandy

Ingredients

1 whole chicken, cut into pieces
3 tablespoons melted butter
1 medium onion, chopped
2 slices bacon
2 well-flavored sweet apples,
    peeled, cored, and cut into thick slices
Salt and pepper
1 cup dry apple cider

Directions

Preheat oven to 350°F (180°C). In a frying pan, brown the chicken all over in the melted butter. Put aside. Sauté the onions, then add the bacon. Increase the heat. As the onions and bacon turn a darker color, add the apples. Shake over a brisk heat. Turn the onion-apple mixture into a casserole, and arrange the chicken pieces on top. Season with salt and pepper. Rinse out the fry pan with the cider and add to the casserole. Cook, covered, for 1½ hours. Yield: 4 servings.

chicken broccoli quiche

Ingredients
½ pound (250 g) broccoli, rinsed
3 eggs
1 cup half and half
¼ teaspoon ground nutmeg
¼ teaspoon ground pepper
1 cup chopped cold cooked chicken
1 cup shredded cheese (Swiss or cheddar)
9-inch pie crust

Directions
Preheat oven to 350°F (180°C). Thinly slice broccoli stalks and cut flowerets into small pieces. Steam or microwave broccoli until tender, about 5 minutes. Let cool. Beat eggs, cream, nutmeg, and pepper together. Spread broccoli, chicken, and cheese evenly in pie shell. Pour egg mixture over the top. Bake until fairly firm, about 45 minutes. Center will jiggle when gently shaken. Cool 15 minutes before serving. Yield: 6 servings.

lemon chicken

Ingredients

3 whole chicken breasts, boned,
   skinned, and halved
1½ cup unbleached flour
⅓ cup butter
2 tablespoons olive oil
Salt and pepper
4 tablespoons butter
4 tablespoons finely chopped parsley
Juice of one lemon

Directions

Preheat oven to 250°F (100°C). Pound chicken breasts flat with a mallet. Melt the butter and oil in a skillet. Put the flour in a plastic bag and shake chicken breasts in flour to coat. Cook the chicken breasts in the skillet over medium-high heat 3 minutes on each side. When finished, salt and pepper them and put into an ovenproof dish. Keep warm in the oven while sauce is made. Add 4 tablespoons butter to the chicken skillet and melt, scraping up brown bits in pan. Remove from heat, then add chopped parsley and the juice from lemon. Pour hot sauce over the breasts and serve with wide egg noodles. Yield: 6 servings.

chicken and rice

Ingredients
4 chicken breasts
½ teaspoon salt
3 tablespoons butter
1 cup raw rice
1 package Spanish rice seasoning mix
1 can (1 pound, 13 ounces) tomatoes, chopped
1 cup water
¼ cup sour cream (optional)

Directions
Preheat oven to 400°F (200°C). Sprinkle chicken with salt. Sauté in butter until golden brown. Put it into a 2-quart casserole. Combine rice and seasoning mix. Sprinkle it evenly around the chicken. Pour the tomatoes and water over all. Cover and bake for 1 hour or until rice is tender and chicken is cooked. Dab tablespoons of sour cream on top of each serving. Yield: 4 servings.

stir-fry chicken

Ingredients
2 whole chicken breasts, skinned
4 green onions, finely chopped
2–3 ounces broccoli, broken into small flowerets
2 medium carrots, scraped and finely sliced lengthwise
4 tablespoons vegetable oil (sesame oil is good for stir fry)
5 tablespoons chicken broth
2 teaspoons light soy sauce
Flour to coat

Directions
With a sharp knife, remove the skin and any bones from the chicken and cut into very thin strips. Dip in flour to coat. Heat 1 tablespoon oil in a large frying pan or wok. When it is very hot throw in the chicken pieces and stir-fry for about 4 minutes, turning constantly. Remove. Heat the remaining oil, then stir fry the prepared vegetables for 3 to 5 minutes on high heat, stirring continuously. Turn heat down and put the chicken pieces back. Add about 2 tablespoons of stock and the soy sauce and stir carefully. Put the lid on and simmer for 2 minutes. Serve on brown or white rice. Yield: 4 servings.

chicken with olives and feta

Ingredients

6 boneless skinless chicken breasts, trimmed and pounded
½ cup, plus 2 tablespoons olive oil
⅓ cup fresh lemon juice
8 teaspoons chopped fresh oregano
2 garlic cloves, pressed
30 pitted kalamata olives, cut into slivers
16 grape tomatoes
½ cup feta cheese, crumbled

Directions

Score tops of chicken breasts with sharp knife and place them in a large glass baking dish. Whisk the ½ cup of oil, lemon juice, 6 teaspoons of oregano, and garlic in a small bowl to blend. Season mixture to taste with salt and pepper. Reserve 3 tablespoons of the mixture for tomatoes. Pour remaining mixture over chicken and turn the chicken to coat well. Cover and refrigerate for at least 3 hours or overnight. Turn occasionally.

Toss olives, tomatoes, feta, remaining 2 teaspoons of oregano, and reserved dressing mixture in a medium bowl. Heat remaining 2 tablespoons of olive oil in a heavy large skillet over medium-high heat. Add chicken and sauté until cooked through, about 3 minutes per side. Transfer to a platter and season with salt and pepper. Spoon tomato mixture over chicken and serve. Yield: 6 servings.

fish

Melt the butter
Dust in flour
Put in drops
Of sweet and sour.

A squeeze of lemon
Pepper too
Add some salt
And stir it through.

Watch it simmer
What a dish
Ooooops!
Don't forget
To add the fish!

sweet and sour fish

Ingredients
1 small can pineapple
1 package frozen fish sticks,
  cooked in oven according to directions
1 tablespoon soy sauce
2 tablespoons vinegar
1 teaspoon ground ginger
2 tablespoons brown sugar
2 tablespoons cornstarch

Directions
Drain pineapple and reserve juice. Add water to juice to make 2 cups of liquid. Cut fish sticks into thirds. In a saucepan, place liquid, soy sauce, vinegar, ginger, brown sugar, and pineapple. Bring to a boil. Mix cornstarch to a smooth paste with a little water. Add to mixture while stirring constantly. Bring to a boil. Simmer for 5 minutes, then add fish pieces. Gently heat through. Serve over fluffy white rice. Yield: 4 servings.

scampi for scamps

Ingredients
1 pound (500 g) fresh medium shrimp
¼ cup butter or margarine
1 tablespoon olive oil
2 teaspoons parsley flakes
½ teaspoon basil flakes
¼ teaspoon oregano
¼ teaspoon garlic powder
¼ teaspoon salt
1 tablespoon lemon juice

Directions
Preheat oven to 450°F (230°C). Peel and devein the shrimp, leaving tail attached. Split each shrimp down the inside lengthwise. Spread open to look like butterflies and then place in a shallow greased baking dish. In a small bowl, melt butter and stir in the remaining ingredients. Pour mixture over shrimp. Bake in the oven for 5 minutes and then place under the broiler for another 5 minutes or until shrimp have flecks of brown. Serve with fluffy rice and steamed vegetables. Yield: 4–6 servings.

rosemary fish and potatoes

Ingredients

1 lb. new potatoes, peeled, washed
   and cut into wedges
4 tablespoons extra virgin olive oil
4 rosemary sprigs
4 whole garlic cloves, peeled
Fine sea salt
Black pepper, freshly ground
2 lb. filet of firm-fleshed fish: groper, red snapper, or mahimahi
2 tablespoons dry, plain breadcrumbs

Directions

Preheat the oven to 400°F (200°C). Place the potato wedges in a baking dish and pour 2 tablespoons of olive oil over them. Add 2 sprigs of rosemary, the garlic cloves, salt, and pepper. Toss thoroughly. Place the dish in the oven. After 15 minutes, remove the dish and turn the potatoes over. Return to oven. Cook for another 10 minutes or until the potatoes feel tender when tested with a fork. Remove the dish from the oven and push the potatoes to the edges to make room in the middle of the dish for the fish to lie flat. Wash the fish fillet, pat it dry with a paper towel, and lay it flat in the dish, skin side down. Strip the leaves from the remaining rosemary sprigs and scatter them over the fish. Add salt and pepper to taste. Sprinkle the breadcrumbs and the remaining 2 tablespoons of oil over the fillet. Return the dish to the oven and bake for 14 minutes. Allow the dish to cool for 3–4 minutes before serving. Yield: 4 servings.

halibut with lemon-lime butter

Ingredients

½ teaspoon lemon zest
½ teaspoon lime zest
2 tablespoons butter or margarine
1½ pounds (750 g) halibut (boneless)

Directions

Stir lemon and lime zest into softened butter. Put mixture on a piece of plastic wrap and roll to form a 1-inch cylinder. Chill in refrigerator. Place fish in a microwave-proof dish with ½ cup water. Cover with plastic wrap. Poke several holes in the plastic and cook for 4 to 6 minutes on high. Turn dish halfway through cooking time. Drain off water and place cooked fish on serving plate. Arrange slices of lemon-lime butter on top of fish. Serve with rice and vegetables. Yield: 4 servings.

Note: Herbed butters are delicious served with baked or steamed fish. Try adding finely chopped parsley or other fresh herbs. Use a butter pat to shape into balls.

smoked trout and white beans

Ingredients
5 tablespoons extra-virgin olive oil
3 tablespoons minced shallot
¼ teaspoon finely grated fresh lemon rind
2 tablespoons fresh lemon juice
½ teaspoon salt
¼ teaspoon black pepper
1 (15–19 oz.) can white beans, rinsed and drained
2 smoked-trout fillets (½ lb. total), skinned and flaked
1 bunch watercress (6 oz.), stems discarded
1 head Bibb lettuce, torn into bite-size pieces

Directions
Bring oil, shallot, lemon rind, juice, salt, and pepper to a simmer in a 2-quart heavy saucepan. Stir in the beans. Remove from the heat and let stand uncovered for 10 minutes to allow the beans to absorb the flavor. In a serving bowl, toss together trout, watercress, lettuce, and bean mixture. Serve while still warm. Yield: 4 servings.

baked crumbed fish

Ingredients
4 fillets of white fish, skinned and boned
2 ounces (55 g) bread crumbs
2 ounces (55 g) grated Parmesan cheese
2 ounces (55 g) butter
1 small tomato

Directions
Preheat oven to 375°F (190°C). Wash fish in cold water, dry and cut into pieces about half-inch square. Spread pieces evenly in shallow ovenproof dish. Put the bread crumbs and cheese in a small bowl and mix well. Rub in the butter by hand until the mixture is even and crumbly. Sprinkle mixture over fish pieces so fish is covered completely. Wash and slice tomato thinly and lay slices of tomato on top of the bread crumbs. Bake for 15 minutes.

shrimp and fish mornay

Ingredients

2 fillets boneless skinless fresh
white fish

8 ounces skimmed milk (or whole
milk with water)

4 ounces small cooked shrimp

1 onion

1 ounce butter

1 tablespoon flour

2 ounces grated cheddar cheese
1 pound (500 g) fettuccine pasta

Crumb Topping

1 tablespoon dry bread crumbs
1 ounce grated cheddar cheese
1 ounce butter

Directions

Preheat oven to 375°F (190°C). Put fish in saucepan with skimmed milk. Bring to boil on high heat, then reduce heat to low and simmer until fish is cooked (about 10 minutes). Drain fish, pouring liquid into small bowl. Break up fish into bite-sized pieces, mixing with shrimps in medium bowl. Melt butter and put chopped onion in saucepan and cook until translucent but not brown. Add flour, stirring briskly, and cook for one minute. Stir liquid from small bowl gradually into saucepan mixing smooth. Once mixture thickens and boils, cook for another 3 minutes. Remove saucepan from heat and stir in cheese. Stir in fish and shrimp. Grease ovenproof dish and pour mixture from saucepan into it. Mix bread crumbs, cheese, and butter in a bowl by hand and sprinkle over top. Cook for 15 minutes. Boil noodles while cooking and serve fish over noodles. Yield: 4 servings.

spinach and apple fish rolls

Ingredients
3 tablespoons butter
1 tablespoon crushed garlic
2 tablespoons parsley, finely chopped
4 fillets white fish, skinned and boned
2 apples, peeled and cut in julienne strips
4 large spinach leaves, blanched and well dried
Juice of 1 lemon

Directions
Mix the butter, garlic, and parsley together to form a paste. Spread about 1 tablespoon over each fish fillet. Divide the apples between the fillets. Roll the fish into tight rolls then wrap each roll in a spinach leaf. Space evenly in a microwave dish and cover with plastic wrap. Microwave on high for 3 to 4 minutes, or until cooked through; test the fish with a skewer—there should be no resistance if the fish is cooked. Spoon over the pan juices and squeeze over the lemon juice. To cook conventionally, place the fish rolls in a baking dish, and dot with butter. Cover and bake at 350°F (180°C) for 15 minutes. Yield: 4 servings.

sole in green noodles

Ingredients
8 ounces green spinach noodles
2 pounds fillet of sole
1½ cups coarsely grated cheddar cheese
1 tablespoon butter
1 can cream of asparagus
   or cheddar cheese soup
1 egg, beaten
1 tablespoon lemon juice
Dash pepper
Paprika

Directions
Preheat oven to 350°F (180°C). Cook noodles in boiling water just until tender; drain and quickly toss with 1 cup grated cheese and butter. Cheese will melt. Place in greased 9x13 Pyrex dish. Lay fillets over the noodles, covering the entire surface. In a small bowl, mix together soup, egg, lemon juice, and pepper. Spoon soup mixture over fish. Sprinkle the remaining ½ cup cheese over the top. Dust with paprika. Bake for 45 minutes. Yield: 8 servings.

creamy crab fettuccine

Ingredients
1 pound (500 g) crab meat, cooked
3 tablespoons butter or margarine
3 tablespoons unbleached flour
½ teaspoon salt
2 cups milk
8 ounces (250 g) fettuccine noodles
Fresh parsley

Directions
Gently heat butter with flour and salt, mixing until smooth. Slowly add milk while stirring constantly to avoid lumps. Allow to boil gently and briefly. Remove from heat and add crab meat and chopped parsley. Keep warm. Cook fettuccine noodles according to packet directions. Drain and rinse. Serve creamy crab sauce over noodles and, if desired, sprinkle with Parmesan cheese. Yield: 4–6 servings.

sam's salmon in foil

Ingredients
1½ pounds fresh salmon
2 tablespoons lemon juice
1 teaspoon all-purpose seasoning mix (Spike)

Directions
Preheat oven to 350°F (180°C). Place salmon on aluminum foil. Brush with lemon juice and sprinkle with seasoning mix. Wrap salmon in foil and seal completely. Place on a roasting tray and cook for 20 minutes. Remove from oven and wait 10 minutes before opening (because of hot steam inside). Serve with a salad and baked potatoes. Yield: 4–6 servings.

Note: Sam, who lives in Seattle, is well-known for this salmon dish. He actually doesn't measure anything, but the results are always delicious.

desserts

*Last night in bed about half-past eleven
in my dream I traveled to Dessert Heaven.
Creamy cakes and luscious bars
were swinging from the moon and stars.
I entered through a delicious gate
and ate and ate and ate.*

chocolate chip cheesecake

Ingredients
1¾ cups graham cracker crumbs
⅓ cup butter
1¼ cups sugar
3 (8 ounce) packages cream cheese, softened
2 teaspoons vanilla extract
3 eggs
1 cup dairy sour cream
1 cup chocolate chips

Directions
Preheat oven to 350°F (180°C). In a bowl, combine crumbs, butter, and
¼ cup sugar. Press on bottom and 1½ inches up side of 8- or 9-inch
springform pan; set aside. In bowl, with electric mixer at high speed,
beat cream cheese, remaining sugar, and vanilla until creamy. Beat in
eggs, one at time. Blend in sour cream and chocolate chips. Spread in
prepared pan. Bake for 60 to 70 minutes or until center is set. Turn off
oven leaving door slightly ajar; leave cheesecake in oven for 1 hour.
Remove from oven; cool completely. Chill 4 hours or overnight, remove
from pan and eat. Yield: 12 servings.

sweet brown rice custard

Ingredients
1 cup granola cereal with raisins
1½ cups cooked brown or white rice
2 cups milk, scalded
2 eggs, lightly beaten
⅓ cup honey or pure maple syrup
2 tablespoons butter or margarine
1 teaspoon vanilla
¼ teaspoon salt
½ teaspoon ground nutmeg

Directions
Preheat oven to 350°F (180°C). Pour cereal into a 1½-quart casserole dish. Add the cooked rice to the scalded milk. Stir in the eggs and remaining ingredients. Pour mixture over cereal. Place the casserole into a shallow pan and pour hot water to 1 inch from the top of the casserole dish. Bake uncovered for 30 minutes. Stir gently and bake 20 minutes, or until a knife inserted in the center comes out clean. Yield: 6 servings.

strawberry pie

Ingredients
Crust
1½ cups unbleached flour
½ teaspoon salt
1 tablespoon sugar
3 tablespoons ice water
⅔ cup soft margarine or shortening

Filling
4 cups strawberries, crushed
1 cup water
¼ cup honey
3 tablespoons cornstarch

Directions
Preheat oven to 350°F (180°C). In a bowl, mix flour, salt, and sugar. Add the margarine and cut into flour until mixture is crumbly. Add water as needed to form a stiff dough. Roll dough on floured surface to form a circle. Gently place in a pie pan and trim edges. Prick bottom and cook for 10 minutes. Simmer 1 cup strawberries with ⅔ cup of water. Mix remaining water with cornstarch. When strawberries come to a boil gradually add cornstarch and stir until mixture is thick and clear. Remove from heat. Put 3 cups of strawberries in pie crust and pour warm strawberry syrup over the top. Chill before serving. Yield: 8 servings.

sour cream apple pie

Ingredients
Double crust for a 9-inch pie
   (Can use double crust recipe from #304 or use your favorite!)
6 cups peeled and thinly sliced baking apples
¾ cup firmly packed light brown sugar
2 teaspoons cinnamon
¼ teaspoon salt
2 tablespoons flour
1 cup sour cream
1 egg, beaten
1 teaspoon vanilla extract
1 teaspoon grated lemon rind

Directions
Preheat oven to 400°F (200°C). Line a 9-inch pie pan with a single crust. Stir together all ingredients except the apples and blend well. Add the apples and toss to coat well. Fill the prepared pie crust and use the remaining crust to make a lattice top. Bake 15 minutes, then reduce heat to 350°F (180°C) and continue baking until the crust is well browned and the apples are tender, 30 to 35 minutes. Yield: 8 servings.

orange bread pudding

Ingredients

10 slices day-old bread, crusts removed, cubed
12-ounce can mandarin oranges, drained
⅓ cup seedless raisins
½ cup chopped almonds (optional)
¼ cup butter, diced
2½ cups milk
3 eggs
⅔ cup brown sugar
½ teaspoon nutmeg
½ teaspoon cinnamon
1 teaspoon vanilla extract
Whipped cream or non-dairy whipped topping

Directions

Preheat oven to 350°F (180°C). Grease a 9x13-inch shallow baking dish. Mix together the bread, oranges, raisins, and nuts. Transfer to the baking pan. In a large bowl, stir together the eggs, sugar, spices, and vanilla. Stir in the milk and butter, then slowly pour onto the bread mixture so that it soaks the bread. Bake for 45 minutes, until set in center and golden brown and crisp on top. Serve with whipped cream or non-dairy whipped topping. Yield: 6–8 servings.

fresh cherry dish

Ingredients
3 cups fresh cherries, pitted
½ cup all-purpose flour
¼ teaspoon salt
4 eggs plus 2 egg yolks
½ cup sugar
2½ cups milk
4 tablespoons melted butter
1 tablespoon powdered sugar

Directions
Preheat the oven to 375°F (190°C). Lightly butter the bottom and sides of a shallow ovenproof dish. Place the cherries in the dish. Sift the flour and salt into a bowl. Add the eggs, egg yolks, sugar, and a little of the milk. Beat into a smooth batter. Gradually beat in the remaining milk and the butter. Strain the batter over the cherries and place the dish in the oven. Bake for 40–50 minutes until golden and firm. Serve warm, dusted with the powdered sugar. Yield: 6 servings.

Note: Use two 15-ounce cans of pitted black cherries, thoroughly drained, if fresh cherries are not available.

honey apples

Ingredients
4 cooking apples
4 tablespoons raisins
⅓ cup liquid honey
1 tablespoon lemon juice
½ teaspoon cinnamon
½ cup water

Directions
Preheat oven to 375°F (190°C). Wash and core the apples and place in a greased baking pan. Loosely fill the center of each apple with raisins and top with a dash of cinnamon. Pour some honey into each apple and allow it to seep down the center. Add lemon juice to water and pour into pan. Stir excess honey into the pan liquid. Bake for 25 minutes or until skin starts to split, basting several times. Can be served with ice cream or custard. Yield: 4 servings.

Note: The best apples for baking whole are Rome Beauties, Granny Smiths, and Pippins. Remember to wash well before using.

fresh peach crisp

Ingredients
8 firm ripe peaches
¼ cup raw sugar or honey
¼ teaspoon salt
1 teaspoon lemon juice
¾ cup unbleached flour
¾ cup brown sugar
½ cup vegetable oil
½ cup chopped walnuts (optional)
½ cup wheat flakes or oat flakes

Directions
Preheat oven to 350°F (180°C). Peel, pit, and slice peaches. Mix with raw sugar and salt. Place a layer of peaches in baking pan and sprinkle with sugar and salt mixture. Repeat layering with all the peaches. Sprinkle with lemon juice. Combine flour, brown sugar, nuts, flakes, and oil to make a crumbly mixture. Spread over peaches. Bake covered for 30 minutes. Remove cover and bake another 15 minutes or until top is browned. Yield: 6 servings.

pineapple meringue fruit salad

Ingredients
½ sweet pineapple, sliced lengthwise
   to retain the green top
2 bananas, peeled and sliced
1 kiwi fruit, peeled and chopped
1 cup mango chunks, or strawberries
2 passion fruits
(Any fruit your children enjoy can work in this dessert,
   you just need enough cut-up fruit to fill the inside of the pineapple)

Meringue
2 egg whites
1 teaspoon apple juice concentrate

Directions
Preheat oven to 400°F (200°C). Using a serrated grapefruit knife, remove flesh from pineapple half, discard core and chop fruit into bite-sized chunks and reserve. Strain off 1/4 cup pineapple juice. Add other fruit and pour pineapple juice over the top. Pile fruit salad into empty pineapple shell. Wrap the green top in foil and place pineapple half on cookie tin. Beat the egg whites until stiff and drizzle in the apple juice concentrate, beat a little longer. Spoon meringue over the fruit carefully bringing it to the edges of the cut pineapple shell and swirling the top and sides, decoratively. Place in oven for approximately 5 minutes or until meringue is lightly browned. Decorate platter with flowers and serve. Yield: 6 servings.

raspberry chocolate tart

Ingredients
2 cups raspberries
½ cup red currant jelly
½ cup non-dairy whipped topping
½ cup milk chocolate chips
1 cup unbleached flour
6 tablespoons softened butter or margarine
6 tablespoons powdered sugar
1 egg yolk
½ teaspoon vanilla extract

Directions
To prepare pastry, sift flour into a bowl and make a hole in the center. Add the egg yolk, sugar, butter, and vanilla. Stir until blended and work into a soft dough. Preheat oven to 350°F (180°C). Press the dough into a greased round cake pan. Bake 12 minutes. Remove from oven and immediately sprinkle the chocolate chips over the hot pastry. Spread evenly. Put jelly in a small saucepan and heat until thin and smooth. Place raspberries over chocolate and pour over the warm jelly. Chill. When ready to serve, top with whipped topping. Yield: 6–8 servings.

banana orange flan

Ingredients
Pastry
1½ cups unbleached flour
6 tablespoons butter
6 tablespoons sugar
3 egg yolks
1 teaspoon vanilla

Filling
¼ cup sugar
2 large oranges
4 ripe bananas
1 cup non-dairy whipped topping or whipped cream

Directions
To make pastry: sift flour into a bowl, make a hole in the center. Add the remaining pastry ingredients and work into a soft dough with fingertips. Chill for 1 hour. Preheat oven to 375°F (190°C). Press dough into a round cake pan and bake 15 minutes. To prepare the filling: put the sugar in a bowl, squeeze the orange juice on top. Slice the bananas into the bowl. After pastry is cool, spoon the bananas onto the dough. Mix the remaining juice into the whipped cream. Spread the whipped cream on top of the bananas and eat! Yield: 8 servings.

fruit gallette

Ingredients
1 pound flaky pastry
4 ounces apricot jam
1 egg, beaten
2 tablespoons powdered sugar

Directions
Preheat oven to 400°F (200°C). Divide pastry in half and roll each half to fit a shallow baking tray. Place one rolled half onto lightly greased tray. Spread jam evenly over top. Using a sharp knife, cut other half of pastry into diagonal half-inch strips leaving an inch border. Gently place this half over the jam. Brush with egg. Bake for 15 to 20 minutes or until golden brown. Remove from oven and drizzle powdered sugar over top. Cool before cutting into squares. Yield: 6–8 servings.

Note: Other jams or jellies can be used for this dessert.

pumpkin steamed pudding

Ingredients
1 cup wholemeal cake flour
½ cup unbleached cake flour
4 teaspoons baking powder
2½ cups wholemeal bread crumbs
2 cups sultanas
2 cups seeded raisins
½ cup roughly chopped dried apricots
½ teaspoon mixed spice
1½ cups pumpkin puree
1½ cups apple juice

Directions
Lightly oil a pudding bowl (a metal bowl will do). In a large bowl, mix the flours, baking powder, bread crumbs, fruit, and spice. In a separate bowl, mix the pumpkin puree and apple juice. Add the liquid ingredients to the dry and combine thoroughly. Put the pudding mixture into the pudding bowl and smooth the top. Place 2 sheets nonstick kitchen paper over the top of the pudding and place lid on firmly. Fill the steamer or large pan with water to come about halfway up the sides of the pudding bowl. Place lid on steamer and bring water to a rolling boil. Reduce the heat, but make sure the water continues to boil rapidly. Steam for 3½ to 5 hours until well set. Make sure to keep checking water level, filling accordingly. Serve with whipped cream. Yield: 10 servings.

strawberry shortcake

Ingredients

1½ pints strawberries, washed, hulled, and halved
3 tablespoons sugar
1 cup whipping cream
Pinch of salt
1 teaspoon sugar
3 tablespoons butter, softened

Shortcakes

⅞ cup unbleached flour
1½ teaspoons sugar
1½ teaspoons baking powder
¼ teaspoon salt
2 tablespoons cold butter
⅜ cup milk

Directions

Combine the strawberries and sugar, toss until well coated, cover, and refrigerate. Preheat oven to 425°F (210°C). Lightly grease a baking sheet. In a large bowl, combine the flour, sugar, baking powder, and salt, then cut in the butter. Stir in the milk and mix until the dry ingredients are just moistened. Do not over mix. On a well-floured work surface, pat the dough to a thickness of ⅜ inch. Using a 3-inch round biscuit cutter, cut out circles of dough and place on greased cookie sheet. Bake for 12 to 15 minutes. Cool. Beat the whipped cream until fluffy, then add the salt and sugar. Cut the shortcakes in half and butter each side. Place the strawberries in the middle and the whipped cream mixture on top. Yield: 6 servings.

blueberry pudding cake

Ingredients
2 cups blueberries
1½ cups unbleached flour
3 teaspoons baking powder
Pinch nutmeg
1 cup pure fruit juice
1 teaspoon vanilla extract
3 egg whites, stiffly beaten

Directions
Preheat oven to 375°F (190°C). Place blueberries in an ovenproof pie dish. Stir flour, baking powder, and nutmeg together in a bowl. Make a well in the center and add juice and vanilla and stir thoroughly to make a stiff batter. Fold in the egg whites. Spoon cake mixture carefully over the fruit. Bake for 40 minutes until top is nicely browned. Serve warm with ice cream or whipped cream. Yield: 6 servings.

Note: Most any fruit could be used in this recipe. Try plums, peaches, pears, strawberries, or apples.

fruit salad cake

Ingredients
1 each: banana, apple, peach
1⅔ cups strawberries
2 pineapple slices
3 tablespoons apricot jam
2 tablespoons brandy or fruit juice
3 tablespoons white wine or fruit juice
½ ounce active dried yeast
2 cups unbleached flour
½ cup butter, melted
4 eggs, separated
⅔ cup sugar
1 teaspoon oil

Directions
Prepare the fruit and cut into small pieces. Place in a large bowl, add the jam, brandy, and wine, stir and leave for one hour. Preheat oven to 400°F (200°C). Sprinkle the yeast over 2 tablespoons warm water and leave until frothy (if yeast doesn't become frothy it is no good, try another pack). Sift flour into bowl and stir in melted butter, egg yolks, sugar, and yeast mixture. Beat hard. Beat the egg whites until they are stiff but not dry. Stir the fruit salad into the dough, then fold in the egg whites. Pour into a greased and floured shallow flan pan. Bake for 40 minutes. Yield: 8 servings.

Note: Use leftover fruit salad in this cake, 3 cups fruit altogether.

blackberry upside-down cake

Ingredients
2½ cups fresh blackberries
½ cup sugar
1 cup all-purpose flour
½ teaspoon baking soda
¼ teaspoon salt
½ stick (2 oz) butter, softened
1 egg
1 teaspoon vanilla
½ cup buttermilk, well stirred

Directions
Preheat oven to 400°F (200°C). Line the bottom of a buttered 8x2-inch round cake pan with 2 rounds of parchment paper; lightly butter parchment. Dust with a little flour and tap off the excess. Arrange the blackberries in a single layer in the cake pan. Sprinkle the berries with 1½ tablespoons sugar. Shake pan to distribute sugar evenly. Sift together the flour, salt, and baking soda and set aside. In a large bowl, beat together butter and remaining ½ cup sugar until light and fluffy. Add egg and vanilla and mix until well blended. Alternately, add the flour mixture and the buttermilk in 3 batches. Mix gently until just blended. Spoon the batter evenly over the blackberries. Bake in the middle of the oven until top is golden and a toothpick comes out clean, 30–35 minutes. Run a thin knife around the edge of the pan then invert onto a large platter. Use pot-holders to hold the plate and pan together as you flip it over. Peel off the parchment. Serve cake warm with ice cream. Yield: 6 servings.

parties

Seems like only yesterday
that he was turning three
bean bag toss and relay races
played around the tree.

Ice cream cones and red balloons
on decorated mats,
funny clowns and magic tricks
pointed birthday hats.

Now I notice posters,
tapes of rock and roll
hot dogs, punch and pretzels,
popcorn in a bowl.

Books on monster movies
skates of black and gray
a cake with baseball figures
he's turning ten today.

time-saving truffle

Ingredients
1 pound cake
2 small packages instant vanilla pudding
4 cups fresh fruit
Non-dairy whipped topping
Fruit jam

Directions
Cut pound cake in half lengthwise. Spread jam in between cake. Cut cake into cubes. Set aside. Make the instant pudding. Prepare fruit, cut into small pieces. Layer in a glass dish, starting with half of the cake cubes, half the pudding, followed by half the fruit. Repeat, ending with fruit on top. Refrigerate until serving. Top with whipped topping if desired. Yield: 8–10 servings.

Question: Describe the best birthday party you could imagine.

cheesy cups

Ingredients
12 slices whole wheat bread
¼ cup butter or margarine
1 cup cheese, grated
3 medium tomatoes

Directions
Preheat oven to 350°F (180°C). Remove crusts from slices of bread. Brush slices with melted butter and press, butter side down, into muffin pans. Bake for 15 minutes or until crisp. Divide cheese among bread cups. Add a slice of tomato and sprinkle with salt and pepper to taste. Return to oven and bake another 10 minutes or until cheese is melted and bubbly. Cool before serving. Yield: 12 servings.

Note: These cups can also be filled with tuna salad, egg salad, or other sandwich spread.

ham or turkey roll-ups

Ingredients
8 ounces (225 g) light cream cheese
1 tablespoon milk
1 pound of sliced boiled ham or turkey

Directions
Beat the cream cheese with milk until light and fluffy. Spread onto the slices of ham or turkey. Roll up like a jelly roll, starting at the narrow end. Wrap in foil and chill. Cut rolls into about 5 pieces. Yield: 50 bite-size pieces.

chocolate-dipped macaroons

Ingredients
1 package (14 oz) flaked coconut
⅔ cup sugar
6 tablespoons flour
¼ teaspoon salt
4 egg whites
1 teaspoon almond extract
1 package (8 squares) baking chocolate, melted

Directions
Preheat oven to 325°F (160°C). Mix coconut, sugar, flour, and salt in a large bowl. Stir in egg whites and almond extract until well blended. Drop by tablespoons, shaped like 2-inch logs, onto greased and floured cookie sheet. Bake for 20 minutes or until the edges are golden brown. Immediately remove from cookie sheet to wire rack. Cool completely. Melt chocolate in a double boiler or over water. Dip the cookies halfway into melted chocolate. Let stand at room temperature or refrigerate on wax paper until chocolate is firm, about 30 minutes. Yield: 24–30.

ice cream cone cakes

Ingredients
Flat bottomed ice cream cones
Cake mix
Frosting mix
Cake decorations
Muffin pan

Directions
Prepare cake mix according to directions. Spoon the batter into the cones until they are ⅔ full. Place the cones on the muffin pan and bake at 350°F (180°C) for 12 to 15 minutes. When cool, frost and decorate. Yield: 12–15 cupcakes.

Activity: Tell your child something about the day he or she was born.

carrot cupcakes

Ingredients

1½ cups sugar
1½ cups vegetable oil
4 eggs
1 cup whole wheat flour
1 cup all-purpose flour
2 teaspoons baking soda
1 teaspoon salt
2 teaspoons ground cinnamon
1 cup grated carrots
1 cup sliced peaches
½ cup chopped walnuts (optional)

Frosting

8 ounces cream cheese, softened
2⅔ cups confectioners' sugar
4 ounces (1 stick) butter or margarine at room temperature
Candied violets (optional) or orange sprinkles for decoration

Directions

Preheat oven to 325°F. To make the cupcakes, mix the sugar, oil, and eggs together until well blended. Sift the dry ingredients together and add to the egg mixture. Mix in the carrots, peaches, and walnuts. Spoon the mixture into well-greased muffin pans to within a half- inch from the top. Bake for 30 minutes or until springy to the touch. Cool on a wire rack. To make the frosting, cream together the cream cheese, confectioners' sugar and butter until smooth. Frost the cupcakes generously and decorate with candied violets or orange sprinkles. Yield: 24 cupcakes.

small stack sandwich

Ingredients
¼ cup butter
⅛ teaspoon salt
1 tablespoon lemon juice
3 ounces (85 g) cream cheese or kefir cheese
5 thin slices of natural white bread
10 thin slices whole grain bread
20 thin tomato slices
20 thin cucumber slices

Directions
Mix together butter, lemon juice, salt, and cream cheese. Using a round cookie cutter, cut 20 circles from the white bread, and 40 circles from the whole wheat bread (you could also use squares and simply cut the crusts off the bread). Spread ½ teaspoon cheese mixture on one side of each bread. To assemble, layer grain bread, tomato, white bread, cucumber, and top with grain bread. Put a toothpick through the sandwich and serve. Yield: 6–8 servings.

fresh flower cake

Ingredients
1 box cake mix
1 large container non-dairy topping
1 large vanilla instant pudding mix
Edible flowers: snapdragons, violas,
  nasturtium, violets, mini roses, carnations,
  pansies, bachelor's buttons, freesia

Directions
Take a box of any kind of cake mix you like. Bake it in two round, square, or heart-shaped pans. When cooled, top with the whipped cream topping. Make pudding according to instructions on box and let jell a few minutes. Mix non-dairy topping with pudding. Ice cake between layers and all around. Top with edible flowers. Very elegant cake for a tea party or girl's birthday.

a cool cake

Ingredients
Favorite cake mix
Vanilla icing
Vegetable food coloring
Corn syrup
Chocolate syrup
5 paper cups

Directions
Bake cake according to package directions. Spread the icing over the cake as smoothly as possible. Pour 2 tablespoons of corn syrup into each of 4 paper cups. Next, add a different food color to each cup and add chocolate syrup to the fifth cup. Drip the colors onto the cake using spoons. Let the colors run together or mix them up and experiment with patterning. Yield: 8 servings.

Note: For an interesting birthday cake, wait until the guests are seated and pass the iced cake around for everyone to decorate!

tiny pineapple burgers

Ingredients
8 ounces tofu, soft
1 pound lean ground beef or turkey
1 cup crushed pineapple, drained
1 tablespoon mustard
1 tablespoon honey, warmed
Whole grain crackers

Directions
In a bowl, soften tofu. Add the ground meat and mix well. Roll into 12 meat-balls and flatten to form small patties. Cook patties in an oiled skillet over medium heat until done, turning once. Blend the honey, mustard, and pineapple together. Place a tiny burger on a cracker. Top with pineapple mixture. Yield: 12 servings.

layered party rice

Ingredients

2⅓ cups long grain white rice
¾ cup butter or margarine
½ cup grated Parmesan cheese
2 eggs
¼ cup grated Swiss cheese
5 slices smoked cooked ham
5 slices mozzarella cheese
¼ teaspoon grated nutmeg
1 teaspoon chopped basil
Salt and pepper to taste

Directions

Boil the rice in salted water until tender. Drain well, place in a bowl, and mix with 6 tablespoons butter, nutmeg, and Parmesan cheese. Preheat oven to 350°F (180°C). Beat the eggs in bowl with the Swiss cheese, salt, pepper, basil, and garlic. Mix well. Melt 2 tablespoons butter into an omelet pan and pour in the egg mixture. Allow to cook until firm, turning over once. Butter a round 10 inch mold. Line the bottom with rice, arrange half the ham on top and place omelet over this, followed by slices of mozzarella and remaining ham. Cover with rice. Dot with butter and bake 15 minutes. Serve hot. Yield: 6 servings.

cream puffs

Ingredients
1 cup water
4 tablespoons butter
1 cup plain flour
3 eggs, beaten
8 ounces whipping cream
2 tablespoons powdered sugar
8 ounces dark chocolate

Directions
Place water and butter in a saucepan and heat until butter is melted and water boils. Remove from heat and add flour stirring vigorously. Return to heat and stir continuously until mixture forms a ball around the spoon. When cool, gradually stir in the eggs, beating well between each addition. Preheat oven to 400°F (200°C). Place teaspoons of the mixture onto greased baking trays. Sprinkle trays with water. Bake puffs for 10 minutes then reduce oven heat to 350°F (180°C) for a further 20 minutes or until golden brown and feel light to the touch. Remove from oven and prick puffs to release steam. Cool.

Whip 5 ounces of the cream until thick and sweeten with powdered sugar. Slit the puffs with a sharp knife and fill with the whipped cream. Melt the chocolate over boiling water. Stir in ⅓ cup of cream and stir until smooth. Spread warm chocolate over each cream puff. Yield: 20 servings.

rainbow jell-o

Ingredients

6 oz. package orange Jell-O
6 oz. package lemon Jell-O
6 oz. package lime Jell-O
6 oz. package cherry Jell-O
4 cups (2 pints) sour cream

Directions

Each step of this recipe is simple, but it takes time for each of the layers to jell, so do this the day before the party. Dissolve the cherry Jell-O in 2 cups boiling water. To ½ cup of the liquefied Jell-O, add 1 cup sour cream and stir well. Pour sour cream mixture into a 9x13-inch glass baking dish and reserve the remaining 1½ cups cherry Jell-O. Put the baking dish on a level shelf in the refrigerator and chill until set. When firm, pour reserved orange Jell-O over creamy layer then chill until firm. Repeat with the remaining colors of Jell-O each with a creamy layer then a clear layer. You may choose whatever order to put the colors in— this could be a good job for the party child.

hot dogs in sleeping bags

Ingredients

1 loaf frozen bread dough, thawed
10 turkey, chicken, or tofu hot dogs
Ketchup, mustard, pickle relish
4 ounces cheddar cheese spread,
   in pressurized can
¼ green pepper, chopped
Corn snack horns

Directions

Divide dough into 10 pieces. On a floured surface, roll each piece into a 10x2-inch rectangle. Place hot dog lengthwise on rectangle. Spread ketchup, mustard and relish on hot dog and roll up so that 1 inch of the hot dog is showing. Pinch edges of dough together. Place on a greased baking sheet. Cover and let rise for 30 minutes. Preheat oven to 375°F (190°C). Bake for 15 minutes or until brown. Cool slightly. Decorate exposed end of hot dog with cheese for hair, green peppers for eyes, and horns for hats. Night, night! Yield: 10 servings.

gift-wrapped sandwiches

Ingredients

12-ounce can chunk light tuna,
   packed in water, drained
⅓ cup mayonnaise (light or regular)
¼ teaspoon salt
1 medium-size carrot
¼ cup dark raisins
8 slices firm wheat bread

Directions

In a medium-size bowl, combine tuna, mayonnaise, and salt. Peel carrot and grate into the tuna mixture. Mix ingredients until well blended then stir in the raisins. With a rolling pin, roll one bread slice until flat, spread evenly with ¼ cup tuna mixture. Roll bread with tuna mixture in a jelly roll fashion. Repeat with remaining bread slices and tuna mixture. Wrap each rolled sandwich in plastic wrap, twisting ends with twist ties or colored ribbons. Or, cover each plastic wrapped sandwich roll with colored tissue paper, twist ends, and tie with ribbons. If not serving right away, keep sandwiches refrigerated or in a cooler. Yield: 8 servings.

ice cream snow balls

Ingredients

3 cups flaked coconut
½ gallon natural vanilla ice cream, or any favorite flavor

Directions

Line a large cookie sheet with waxed paper. Make ice cream into 16 separate balls. Place on cookie sheet and freeze until firm. Put coconut on a plate and remove ice cream balls from freezer. Quickly roll each ball in coconut and return to freeze until firm. Yield: 6–8 snow balls.

Note: Children's appetites vary from day to day. Vary your menus, but keep them nutritious and appealing.

tea party snacks

Ingredients
3 hard-boiled eggs
⅔ cup crushed pineapple
½ cup cottage cheese
Salt and pepper
Savory crackers
Butter for spreading

Directions
Chop hard-boiled eggs and mix with pineapple, cottage cheese, salt and pepper. Spread crisp savory crackers with butter and top with egg and pineapple spread. Serve with beverage in small tea cups.

holidays

Ghosts and goblins
pumpkins too
steaming pots
of witches brew.

Scary music
tricks and treats
cheerful chatter
bags of sweets.

Haunted houses
shrieks of fright
it's Halloween
Our favorite night!

queen of hearts tarts

Ingredients
2 cups unbleached flour
2 tablespoons powdered sugar
4 tablespoons butter or margarine
Pinch of salt
2½ tablespoons cold water
4 ounces jam, naturally sweetened

Directions
Preheat oven to 425°F (180°C). Sift flour, sugar, and salt into a bowl. Cut the butter into the flour with tips of fingers, making fine crumbs. Sprinkle water over mixture and mix to a smooth, stiff dough. Roll out dough on a floured surface to about ¼-inch thick. Cut into rounds a bit larger than the muffin tins. Press each round into greased muffin holes. Put a tablespoon of jam on each round. Bake 12 minutes or until tarts are light brown. If desired, drizzle with powdered sugar before serving. Yield: 12 tarts.

shamrock butter cookies

Ingredients

8 ounces (225 g) butter, softened
4 ounces (125 g) fine sugar
10 ounces (275 g) unbleached flour
4 tablespoons fine semolina
4 ounces (100 g) confectioners sugar
1 tablespoon warm water
Green food coloring

Directions

Preheat oven to 350°F (180°C). In a bowl, beat the butter and sugar together until creamy. Stir in the flour and semolina and knead. Form into a ball and roll out on a floured surface to about ¼-inch thick. Using shamrock cookie cutter, cut out shapes (or place 3 small circles together and attach a triangle at the base). Bake for 15 minutes or until light brown and then cool on a wire rack. Make the frosting by combining the confectioners sugar and water, beating well until the mixture is smooth. Add a drop of green coloring and blend. Frost the cookies to within ¼-inch of edge. Yield: 12 cookies.

easter egg braid

Ingredients

2 packages active dry yeast
1 teaspoon honey
¼ cup warm water
6 cups unbleached flour
1 teaspoon salt
2 cups warm water
3 eggs, beaten

¼ cup vegetable oil
3 tablespoons honey
8 raw, decorated eggs
1 egg yolk
1 tablespoon milk

Directions

Combine first 3 ingredients. Measure flour and salt into a bowl. Make a well and add the water, beaten eggs, vegetable oil, honey, and yeast mixture. Beat well until a ball of dough is formed, then turn out onto a floured board and knead for 10 minutes until smooth and elastic. Place in a greased bowl, cover, and allow to rise until doubled in bulk (about one hour). Punch down and divide dough into two sections. Cut each section of dough into 3 parts and roll between hands into long cylinders. With the three ropes of dough lying side by side, start to braid loosely, inserting raw decorated eggs every now and then. Finish the ends by tucking them under. Repeat for the second loaf. Cover and let rise until almost doubled in bulk. Brush tops with 1 egg yolk diluted with 1 tablespoon milk. Bake 15 minutes in a 400°F (200°C) oven. Reduce heat to 375°F (190°C) and bake for 45 minutes. Yield: 10 servings.

christmas wreaths

Ingredients
36 large marshmallows (one large bag)
½ cup butter
½ teaspoon vanilla
3½ cups corn flakes
¼ teaspoon green food coloring
1 package candy red hots

Directions
Over medium heat, melt the marshmallows and butter together. Stir in vanilla and food coloring. Fold in the corn flakes and mix well. Drop by tablespoons onto waxed paper. Butter workers' fingers (a good job for small hands) and form into little wreaths. Decorate with candies. These will become firm as they cool. For quick firming, put in refrigerator fo 30 minutes.

mother's day soufflé

Ingredients
1 loaf white bread (sourdough is good)
2 cups grated cheese
Ham or bacon bits to taste
12 eggs
1 cup milk
Seasonings, if desired

...efore. Cut crusts off bread and slice
...n pan. Place one layer of bread on
...and ham. Place remaining bread on
...s together. Pour over the top of the
...n a preheated 350°F (180°C) oven
...erve with a fresh fruit salad. Yield:

...ot only to give mother breakfast in
... family so that she can stay in bed.

dad's favorite chocolate cherry coffee cake

Ingredients
½ teaspoon salt
1½ teaspoons baking soda
1¾ teaspoons baking powder
3¼ cups whole wheat pastry flour
1 cup butter
1½ cups honey
2¼ teaspoons vanilla
3 eggs
1½ cups sour cream
4 ounces unsweetened baker's chocolate, melted
1¼ cups pitted cherries, fresh or canned

Directions
Preheat oven to 350°F (180°C). Grease a tube pan. Sift dry ingredients together and set aside. Cream the butter and honey and add vanilla. Add eggs one at a time, beating well after each. Add the dry ingredients alternately with the sour cream. Drain the cherries well, then stir into batter along with the melted chocolate. Bake for 50 to 60 minutes or until a knife inserted in the center of the cake comes out clean.

fourth of july fruit plate

Ingredients
2 cups frozen whipped topping, thawed
2 cups natural low-fat vanilla yogurt
½ teaspoon nutmeg
½ teaspoon vanilla extract
1 watermelon, sliced
6 cups blueberries

Directions
Combine whipped topping, yogurt, nutmeg and vanilla. Chill until serving time. Cut watermelon slices into triangular wedges. Place the bowl of topping in the middle of a large plate. Arrange the blueberries around the bowl. Finally, place the watermelon wedges, tips out, on edge of plate to form a star effect. To serve, dip fruit into topping and enjoy. Yield: 6–8 servings.

Note: Ants are allergic to white chalk. To keep them away from food on your Fourth of July picnic, draw lines along the edges of the picnic table with white chalk.

caramel apple bobs

Ingredients
Bag of caramels, unwrapped
6 apples, cut into small pieces

Directions
Heat caramels over low heat. Add 1 or 2 tablespoons water to thin caramels to desired consistency. Pour over cut apples and eat! Yield: 4–6 servings.

Note: Have children play a bobbing-for-apples game before you cut up the apples for dessert. Get a big shallow tub of water and put the apples in it. Tie child's hands behind their backs and have them bob for the apples in the water, trying to pick up apples with their teeth. Make sure you are close by to supervise!

roast turkey with fruit stuffing

Ingredients
12–16 pound turkey, ready to stuff
1 cup apple jelly
1 package mixed dried fruit
1 medium onion, minced
1 package cranberries
½ cup honey
5 cups day-old bread crumbs
1 teaspoon salt
½ teaspoon ground allspice

Directions
Remove giblets and neck from cavity of turkey. Rinse with running water, drain and pat dry. Preheat oven to 325°F (170°C). To make stuffing, boil 2 cups of water in a saucepan. Add dried fruit and onion. Reduce heat and simmer for 15 minutes or until fruit is tender. Place mixture in a large bowl. In same saucepan, heat ¼ cup water and add cranberries and honey. Bring to a boil and then simmer for 7 minutes, stirring. Remove from heat and drain. Add berries to fruit mixture. Add bread crumbs, salt, and allspice and toss lightly. Spoon some stuffing into neck cavity. Fold neck skin over and secure. Spoon remaining stuffing into body cavity and close by folding skin over opening and securing. Roast, breast side up, for 4 to 4½ hours. During last 20 minutes, brush turkey with warmed apple jelly several times. Yield: 12–18 servings.

fall pumpkin soup

Ingredients
3–4 pound pumpkin
1 tablespoon butter
¼ cup finely minced onion
1 teaspoon prepared mustard
13 ounce can low-fat evaporated milk
2 slices rye bread, cubed
Salt, pepper, nutmeg to taste
½ cup (packed) grated Swiss cheese

Directions
Preheat oven to 350°F (180°C). Prepare the pumpkin as if you were going to make a jack-o'-lantern (cut off top and scoop out seeds and strings). Rub the inside of the pumpkin with the soft butter. Add all the remaining ingredients. Cover the top of the pumpkin with tin foil before replacing the lid. Place the pumpkin tureen on a tray and place the tray in the oven. Bake until the pumpkin becomes tender (about 2 hours). To serve, scoop deeply into the pumpkin to bring pieces from the sides and bottom into the soup. Yield: 4–6 servings.

challah breakfast toast with berry sauce

Ingredients

3 large eggs
1 cup whole milk
1 teaspoon sugar
¼ teaspoon salt
1 (1 lb.) challah loaf
2 oz unsalted butter

Berry Sauce
3 cups mixed berries: blackberries, raspberries, blueberries
½ cup sugar
1 tablespoon fresh lemon juice

Directions

Cut the challah loaf crosswise into 12 half-inch thick slices, not including the end pieces. Whisk together eggs, milk, sugar, and salt until well blended. Pour mixture into a large baking pan and soak bread slices in a single layer, turning once. Heat half of the butter in a 12-inch heavy skillet over moderately high heat until foam subsides. Transfer four soaked bread slices to skillet with a slotted spatula and cook until golden brown, about 1 minute on each side. Cook remaining bread slices, adding more butter as needed. Keep cooked slices in a warm oven. Serve the Breakfast Toast with the Berry Sauce and dust with powdered sugar. Yield: 4 servings.

Berry Sauce

Puree one and a half cups of the berries with sugar and lemon juice in a blender. To eliminate seeds, force puree through a fine sieve into a bowl. Transfer puree to a serving bowl and fold in remaining berries.

spring young garlic soup

Ingredients

1 tablespoon extra-virgin olive oil
½ pound fresh young garlic bulbs, roughly chopped
1 small yellow onion, peeled and diced
1 stalk celery, peeled and diced
3 Yukon Gold potatoes, peeled and diced
2 quarts (8 cups) chicken of vegetable stock
¼ teaspoon cayenne pepper
1 cup whipping cream
1 teaspoon salt
¼ teaspoon pepper
1 sprig fresh thyme, leaves only
¼ cup sour cream or plain yogurt
¼ pound pea shoots or chopped watercress

Directions

In a large, heavy saucepan heat the olive oil over medium heat. Add the garlic, onion, and celery and cook for 5 minutes, stirring constantly. Add the potatoes, stock, cayenne pepper, and whipping cream. Just before the mixture comes to a boil, lower the heat and allow to simmer for 20 minutes or until the potatoes are tender. Add salt, pepper, and thyme. Remove from heat and puree in a blender. Strain the soup through a fine mesh sieve and adjust seasonings to taste. Serve in bowls or cups while still warm. Garnish with dollops of sour cream or plain yogurt and pea shoots. Yield: 6–8.

Note: This soup can also be served chilled.

snow balls

Ingredients
1 cup butter, softened
¾ cup sugar
2 cups natural white flour
8-ounce bag of chocolate kisses
Powdered sugar for dusting

Directions
Preheat oven to 350°F (180°C). Cream butter and sugar until smooth then add flour. Wrap in plastic and refrigerate for half an hour. In the meantime, remove foil from the chocolate kisses (a good job for little elves). Remove dough from refrigerator and shape into 1-inch round balls. Insert kiss into center of ball, making sure it is completely covered by dough. Bake on ungreased baking sheet for 10 to 12 minutes. Sift powdered sugar over the top while still warm. Yield: 24 cookies.

world dishes

*Turn on the music
dim the lights low
light the pretty candles
knead out the dough
cook spicy pasta
on a plate piled high
then serve alongside
a fat pizza pie.
Feel like a restaurant
in the city of Rome
without having to travel
far from home.*

filipino fried egg rolls

Ingredients
½ pound ground lean pork
½ pound shrimp, deveined, cooked and chopped
½ cup water chestnuts, chopped fine
1 bunch green onions, chopped fine
1 teaspoon salt
½ teaspoon black pepper
1 egg
1 tablespoon soy sauce
1 packet Lumpia wrappers or egg roll wrappers
½ cup vegetable oil

Directions
In a medium-size bowl, mix together the pork, shrimp, water chestnuts, green onions, beaten egg, and soy sauce. Season the mixture with salt and pepper. Place a tablespoon of the filling on each wrapper. Fold the wrapper over the filling, burrito style, tucking in the ends. Heat the oil over medium heat in a heavy fry pan or wok. Fry the egg rolls until golden brown, turning to cook all sides. Serve with steamed rice or as a finger food. Yield: 4–6 servings.

jamaican papaya shrimp

Ingredients

3 tablespoons butter
2 cloves of garlic, minced
1 small onion, peeled and chopped
1 sprig fresh thyme, leaves only,
   or 1 teaspoon dried thyme
1 pound medium shrimp, deveined
½ medium papaya, seeded, peeled,
   and chopped into ½-inch chunks

Directions

Melt the butter in a heavy saucepan over medium heat. Saute the garlic and onion until light brown. Add the papaya and thyme and stir until the papaya just begins to get soft and mushy. Remove from heat and spoon the mixture into a bowl. Saute the shrimp in the same saucepan, adding more butter if necessary, for 3–5 minutes. Fold the papaya mixture into the shrimp and heat through on low heat until shrimp are fully cooked. Serve over steamed rice or noodles. Yield: 4 servings.

french onion soup

Ingredients
¼ cup butter or margarine
3 large onions, peeled and sliced
1 tablespoon flour
2½ cups water
2 10½-ounce cans beef broth
1 loaf French bread
1 cup Swiss cheese, grated

Directions
Preheat oven to 325°F (170°C). In a saucepan over medium heat, cook onions in butter until soft (about 10 minutes). Stir in flour until blended and slowly add water and beef broth. Heat to boiling. Reduce heat and simmer covered for 10 minutes. Cut four 1-inch slices of bread and toast in the oven until lightly brown, 10 minutes. Ladle soup into 4 ramekin bowls and place slice of toasted bread on top. Sprinkle ¼ of the cheese over each slice of bread. Place bowls in oven at 425°F (220°C) for 10 minutes or until cheese is melted. Cool bowls before serving to children. Yield: 4 servings.

nasi goreng

Ingredients
1 package frozen peas and carrots
1 pound pork or chicken
2 tablespoons vegetable oil
1 onion, peeled and chopped
4 cups cooked rice
2 tablespoons soy sauce
¼ teaspoon sage
Pepper and salt to taste
1 egg, beaten

Directions
Cook the peas and carrots, drain and set aside. Cut meat into very small pieces. Melt 2 tablespoons oil or butter in a frying pan. Add meat and onions and brown. Add rice, soy sauce, sage, salt, and pepper. Cook slowly and stir frequently for 15 minutes. Add peas and carrots and cook for another 5 minutes. In a small frying pan, cook the egg so it is flat like a pancake. Cut egg mixture into strips and lightly mix into the rice mixture. Serve with slices of tomato and cucumber. Yield: 6 servings.

Note: Nasi Goreng comes from the Dutch East Indies which is now called Indonesia. It is also a favorite in Malaysia.

greek potato salad

Ingredients

2 pounds (900 g) small potatoes, unpeeled, halved crossways if large
1 medium red onion, very thinly sliced
1 yellow pepper, cored, seeded and thinly sliced
1 red or green pepper, cored, seeded and thinly sliced
6 ounces (175 g) feta cheese, crumbled
2 tomatoes seeded and cut into eighths
3 ounces (90 g) Greek Kalamata olives, rinsed, stoned, and halved

Dressing

4 ounces (125 ml) lemon juice
4 ounces (125 ml) olive oil
2 cloves garlic, crushed
1½ tablespoons chopped fresh mint
1 tablespoon oregano
Salt and pepper to taste

Directions

Steam potatoes until tender. Drain in a colander under cool running water. Allow to cool to room temperature. Meanwhile, prepare the dressing in a non-metallic bowl. Whisk together the lemon juice, olive oil, garlic, mint and oregano until well blended. Season with salt and pepper. To assemble the salad, toss together the potatoes and half of the dressing and leave the potatoes to cool completely. Add the onion, peppers, feta cheese, tomatoes, and olives to the remaining dressing and toss into the potatoes. Serve. Yield: 6–8 servings.

scotch eggs

Ingredients
1 pound (500 g) ground beef or pork
1 cup bread or cracker crumbs
1 tablespoon tomato or steak sauce
5 eggs
½ onion, minced

Directions
Preheat oven to 350°F (180°C). Hard-boil 4 eggs and remove shells. Mix together the meat, ½ cup bread crumbs, sauce, onion, and remaining egg. If too dry, add water or milk one tablespoon at a time. Season with salt and pepper. Divide the mixture into fourths and roll from into balls. Flatten each portion to make a circle about the size of a saucer. Place a hardboiled egg in the center of the circle and fold the meat to completely cover the egg. Roll in remaining breadcrumbs. Bake in a greased roasting dish for 30 minutes, turning once or twice. To serve, cut in half and garnish with a sprig of fresh parsley. Yield: 8 servings.

Note: Bake potatoes in the same dish as the Scotch Eggs and serve with broiled tomatoes—halved and topped generously with grated Parmesan cheese.

new zealand pavlova

Ingredients
4 egg whites
¼ teaspoon salt
1 cup sugar
4 teaspoons cornstarch
2 teaspoons vinegar
1 teaspoon vanilla
3 cups diced tropical fruit:
    bananas, kiwis, pineapple, etc.
1 cup whipping cream or non-dairy whipped topping

Directions
Preheat oven to 275°F (140°C). Grease and flour a round cake pan. Whip the egg whites with salt until they hold a stiff peak. Add the sugar, one teaspoon at a time, beating until the mixture is stiff and shiny. Beat in the cornstarch, vinegar and vanilla. Put the meringue mixture into the shallow cake pan and hollow out the middle so the edges are about a half-inch above the middle. Bake for 1¼ hours or until the meringue is light brown. Cool completely and cover with whipped cream and fruit. Yield: 10–12 servings.

pirate's paella from spain

Ingredients

4 chicken breasts, boned and cut
1 onion, chopped
1 green pepper, chopped
2 tomatoes, peeled and chopped
½ teaspoon saffron or turmeric
2 cloves garlic, crushed
Salt and pepper to taste
2 cups long grain rice

4 cups chicken broth
1 pound (500 g) cooked
  shrimp
1 cup frozen peas

Directions

In a skillet or frying pan, brown chicken in 3 tablespoons vegetable oil over medium heat until golden. Remove from pan. Add onion and stir until brown. Add green pepper, tomatoes, saffron, garlic, and salt and pepper to taste. Simmer for 5 minutes, stirring occasionally. Add rice, chicken, and shrimp. Pour chicken broth over mixture and stir lightly. Cover and cook on low for 50 minutes. Sprinkle peas over top, cover and cook another 10 minutes or until liquid is absorbed and rice is tender. Yield: 8 servings.

Note: Paella is a saffron-flavored dish from Spain made with varying combinations of rice, vegetables, meat, and seafood. The word "paella" means pan in Old Spanish. If your children like shellfish, you can add clams or mussels.

flat bread from india

Ingredients
1 cup whole wheat flour
1 cup unbleached white flour
¼ teaspoon salt
1 tablespoon butter

Directions
Sift the flours and salt together. Stir in ½ cup water and the butter. Knead to make a stiff dough. Let the dough stand uncovered for an hour. Form into small balls the size of walnuts. Roll each dough ball into very thin circles on a floured board. Bake on a preheated griddle or frying pan over low heat. Turn chapatis often until both sides are light brown, but not hard. Serve with curry or stew. Yield: 12.

Note: The Indians of India use chapatis instead of utensils. Let your child try this way of eating—scooping the food up with a chapati.

oriental stir fry

Ingredients

1 pound lean pork or chicken
1 bunch bok choy
1 small can water chestnuts
1 cup fresh mushrooms
3 green onions
1 tablespoon vegetable oil

Sauce

1 cup chicken broth
¼ cup soy sauce
2 tablespoons dry sherry
2 tablespoons cornstarch
¼ teaspoon garlic powder
¼ teaspoon ground ginger

Directions

Cut pork or chicken into ¼-inch strips. Slice bok choy, water chestnuts, mushrooms, and onions. Heat oil in wok or frying pan. Add pork to hot oil and stir-fry 3 to 5 minutes until light brown. Remove to a plate. Add vegetables to wok and stir-fry 4 to 5 minutes. Combine sauce ingredients. Pour over vegetables in wok. Add pork or chicken and heat through for about 3 minutes stirring constantly, until thickened. Serve over rice or noodles. Yield: 4–6 servings.

Note: Use this meal to learn how to use chopsticks. The Chinese word for chopsticks is kwai-tsze and means "quick ones" because food can be eaten more quickly if you don't have to cut it up first.

australian cabbage salad

Ingredients

2 cups finely shredded cabbage (half a medium head)

1 fresh pineapple, peeled, cored and cubed or 1 15-ounce can in own juice

1 orange, peeled and separated or cut into segments

1 grapefruit, peeled and separated or cut into segments

1 small cucumber, peeled and thinly sliced

1 red bell pepper, seeded and sliced into strips

1 cup finely chopped ham

Directions

Place all ingredients—cabbage, pineapple, orange, grapefruit, cucumber, red pepper, and ham—into a large salad bowl and toss gently until blended with salad servers. Chill in the refrigerator while preparing the salad dressing.

Dressing

1 tablespoon grated orange rind

4 tablespoons virgin olive oil or other vegetable oil

2 tablespoons apple cider vinegar

2 tablespoons mayonnaise

2 tablespoons heavy whipping cream

Salt and pepper to taste

Place all ingredients into a small bowl and whisk together until blended. Add a teaspoon of honey or sugar if the taste is too sour. Pour the dressing over the salad and stir gently to blend. Serve on lettuce leaves on individual plates. Yield: 4–6.

botswanan plantain chips

Ingredients
6 green or yellow plantains
2 cups vegetable oil
Salt to taste

Directions
Peel the plantains by cutting through the skin lengthwise and opening with fingers. Slice the peeled plantains diagonally into ¼-inch oval slices. Heat ½ cup of oil in a heavy skillet over medium heat. Fry the plantain slices a few at a time, turning frequently until golden brown, about 5 minutes total. Using a slotted spoon, remove chips from skillet and drain on paper towels. Add more oil to the skillet as necessary and continue to cook the slices in small batches until all are fried. Sprinkle the chips with salt to taste. Chips can be served hot or cold as snacks or as an accompaniment to meals. Yield: 4–6 servings.

Note: In Botswana, a country known for its vast savanna land and its precious minerals, these plantain chips are called dodo.

cornish pasties

Ingredients

3 cups unbleached flour
¼ teaspoon salt
½ cup butter
8 tablespoons cold water
½ pound (250 g) lean beef
½ teaspoon salt
1 small potato, peeled
1 carrot, chopped
1 small onion, chopped
½ cup peas
1 egg white, slightly beaten

Directions

Preheat oven to 450°F (230°C). Make pastry by sifting together flour and salt and rubbing in the butter until mixture is crumbly. Add enough cold water to form dough into a ball. Chill. Mix meat and potato. Combine with other vegetables. Roll out pastry very thin and cut out 8 circles, 6 inches in diameter. Spoon ⅛ of the filling onto the center of each circle. Dampen edges, then fold pastry in half. Crimp edges to seal. Brush with egg white. Slash pastry to allow steam to escape. Bake for 10 minutes. Reduce heat to 350°F (180°C) and bake for 30 more minutes or until pastry is golden brown. Cool 10 minutes before serving. Yield: 8 servings.

russian kasha

Ingredients

2 cups broth, consommé, or bouillon
½ teaspoon salt
¼ teaspoon pepper
2 tablespoons butter
1 egg, slightly beaten
1 cup buckwheat or Kasha

Directions

Combine the broth, salt, pepper, and butter in a saucepan and bring to a boil. In a bowl, mix together the beaten egg and buckwheat until all the kernels are moistened. Place the kernels in a frying pan and cook on high heat, stirring constantly, until kernels are dry and separate. Reduce heat to low and steam kernels for 10 minutes. Remove cover, fluff with a fork, and serve warm. Yield: 6 servings.

Note: Kasha, also known as buckwheat or groats, is a fine source of protein. It is a favorite food of Russian children.

italian chicken risotto

Ingredients
¼ cup minced onion
2 tablespoons olive or vegetable oil
3 tablespoons butter
1½ cups uncooked rice
4 cups chicken stock
1½ cups cooked and shredded chicken
½ cup Parmesan cheese

Directions
Lightly brown the onion in heated oil and butter. Add rice and stir until the rice turns white. Add the stock slowly, stirring frequently. Keep the mixture bubbling as the stock is added. Stir in the chicken with the last of the stock. When the rice is done, in 20 to 30 minutes, stir in the cheese. Season with salt and pepper and serve immediately. Sprinkle with additional Parmesan cheese if desired. Yield: 6–8 servings.

Note: This recipe is also good with leftover cooked turkey.

quesadillas

Ingredients
3 six-inch (150 mm) flour tortillas
Vegetable cooking oil or butter
1 cup shredded white cheese
1 cup shredded yellow cheese
½ cup finely chopped tomato
Parsley or cilantro leaves

Directions
Lightly fry each tortilla in oil or butter over medium heat until crisp and golden, turning once. While in frying pan, sprinkle with combined cheeses and top with tomato. Cover with lid for a few minutes until cheese is melted. Fold in half and remove from frying pan. Cut in half and garnish with parsley or cilantro leaves. Serve warm. Yield: 3 servings.

Note: If using conventional oven, place tortillas on a cookie sheet and bake at 350°F (180°C) for 10 minutes or until cheese is melted.

brazilian flan

Ingredients
1 can (14 oz) sweetened condensed milk
3 eggs
2 cups milk
1 cup sugar

Directions
Preheat oven to 325°F (160°C). Lightly grease a 9-inch pie dish. Place sugar in a small heavy saucepan over medium heat. Stir constantly until the sugar melts and becomes caramel colored. Pour the warm sugar liquid into the pie plate and swirl until the bottom is evenly coated. Set aside. Place the condensed milk, eggs, and milk in a blender and mix until smooth or use a whisk to beat the ingredients together in a medium bowl. Pour the mixture into the pie dish. Place the pie dish in a roasting pan and add water to the pan until it reaches half way up the sides of the pie dish. Bake for 90 minutes in a moderate oven or until a knife inserted in the center comes out clean. Remove pie dish from roasting pan and cool to room temperature. Refrigerate at least 4 hours or overnight, before serving. Invert onto a large serving plate. Yield: 6–8 slices.

Note: To release the flan from the pie dish, first run a table knife around the edge of the dish. Invert the serving plate over the pie dish. Turn over and shake gently to release the flan. The more chilled the flan, the easier it is to release.

I've now learned what nutrition means
it's saying "good-bye" to jelly beans
good-bye to hidden candy bars
to drawers stuffed with chocolate bars
to donut holes, to sugar pops
to potato chips and lemon drops.
It's saying "hello" to raisins
mixed granola in a bowl
to apples topped with cinnamon
fresh honey on a roll!

Conversion Table

Liquid or Dry Ingredients

¼ cup = 60 ml
⅓ cup = 80 ml
½ cup = 125 ml
¾ cup = 190 ml
1 cup = 250 ml
2 cups = 500 ml

¼ teaspoon = 1.5 ml
½ teaspoon = 3 ml
1 teaspoon = 5 ml
3 teaspoons = 15 ml
1 tablespoon = 15 ml

1 inch = 25 mm
½ inch = 12 mm
¼ inch = 6 mm

Temperatures

250°F = 120°C
275°F = 140°C
300°F = 150°C
325°F = 160°C
350°F = 180°C
375°F = 190°C
400°F = 200°C
425°F = 220°C
450°F = 230°C

Weights

1 ounce = 30 grams
4 ounces = 125 grams
8 ounces = 250 grams
16 ounces = 500 grams
2 pounds = 1 kilogram

Special Thanks

A special thanks to Ormandale School in Portola Valley, California. To the teachers, Earlyne Mund, Kathy Kobara, and Sue Stewart, and especially to the children who illustrated our recipes.

Thanks also to the children in Christchurch, New Zealand, for their diligence, care, and artistry they demonstrated in their renderings of fruits, vegetables, and animal life.

David Nelligan
Sandy Ballentine
James ⌗ Koblick
Allison C. Wagner
Joshua McLaren
NANI WICKSTEE
Sharon Terwilliger
Kristin Lucco
Ali Rasch
Jay Ritchey
@MATT*Skrabo
Suzanne Dayeh
Sean Bleier
Missy Woodrow
Matt Laws
Daniel Silberman
GEORGINA cool Georgina Chambers !!!
Devon Watts!
Jeffrey Frey
Riley Bradley
Jessica Kornberg
Joshua Sternbach
Ryan Forster
Lucinda Lannie
Kelly Nichols
Daniel Mazawa
Micah Johnson
Julie Falconer
Justin Martin
tyler Bushnell
Julie Castello
Shane Sykes
Matt Kanzler
Lauren Rosenthal
Vanessa Salsbury
Ryan Piaget
Kate Parmer
Becky Latter
Stephanie Balogh
Jenny Bond
Margaret Ward
Rachel ☕ Samuels

Peter Bergman

Brooke Ellison Rebecca Sternbach Maria Macolin Ted Conrad! Paul

Nick cOnrad NIKOS Amanda O. Conradt Wagner
              Hunner

Trevor F. Crane

Wesley Ellison Morgan ?, Jackson. Paul*Oikawa Mike Katz

Kimberly Nicky Intersimone

Penny Conaghan Epprecht Rachel Saal

Rhett Ellison

About the Authors

Sheila Ellison has a BA degree in psychology from the University of Southern California, and is the creator and author of the very popular and successful 365 series of parenting books, including *365 Days of Creative Play* and *365 Afterschool Activities*. These books have grown out of Sheila's lifelong involvement with children, her many volunteer efforts on their behalf, and her founding of community youth groups and mentoring programs. The mother of four children, she has recently completed national media tours presenting her ideas on successful parenting along with new products that make life with children easier. She is currently writing her next work.

Dr. Judith Gray is internationally known as an author, teacher, leader in dance research, and speaker on future trends in education. A former Executive Director of the Girls Club of Tucson, Dr. Gray has been an educator at both the high school and university levels. A mother of four, she is currently helping to develop state-of-the-art high schools in Washington and is on the Antioch University teaching faculty. Dr. Gray is also the coauthor of *365 Days of Creative Play* and *365 Afterschool Activities* and has also published three books on dance.

Hungry for More Child-Care Tips?
Don't Miss

365 Days of Creative Play

For Children Two Years and Up
by Sheila Ellison and Dr. Judith Gray

365 Days of Creative Play is the essential guide to a wide variety of creative projects for young children.

"Activities that may work magic: projects that you can do with your kids, and even better, activities that they can do all by themselves."

—*Family Circle Magazine*

Written by the authors of *365 Foods Kids Love to Eat*, *365 Days of Creative Play* will encourage your child's imagination, growth, and problem solving skills.

416 pages, ISBN: 1-4022-0535-X, $8.95.

Notes

_____

_____

_____

_____

_____

_____

_____

_____

_____

_____

_____

_____

Notes

Notes

_____

_____

_____

_____

_____

_____

_____

_____

_____

_____

_____

_____

Notes

Notes

Notes

Notes

Notes

_____

_____

_____

_____

_____

_____

_____

_____

_____

_____

_____

_____

Notes

Notes

_____

_____

_____

_____

_____

_____

_____

_____

_____

_____

_____

_____

Notes